DAVID
COULTHARD

Patrick Stephens Limited, an imprint of Haynes Publishing, has published authoritative, quality books for more than a quarter of a century. During that time the company has established a reputation as one of the world's leading publishers of books on aviation, maritime, motor cycle, car, motorsport, and railway subjects. Readers or authors with suggestions for books they would like to see published are invited to write to: The Editorial Director, Patrick Stephens Limited, Sparkford, Nr Yeovil, Somerset BA22 7JJ.

DAVID
COULTHARD

THE FLYING SCOTSMAN

Jim Dunn

PSL

Patrick Stephens Limited

First published in 1995

British Library Cataloguing-in-Publication Data:
A catalogue record for this book is
available from the British Library

ISBN: 1 85260 530 8

Library of Congress catalog card no. 95 76126

Patrick Stephens Limited is an imprint of Haynes Publishing,
Sparkford, Nr Yeovil, Somerset BA22 7JJ.

Designed and typeset by G&M, Raunds, Northamptonshire
Printed in Britain by Butler & Tanner Ltd, London and Frome

Contents

Acknowledgements

I WOULD LIKE to thank the Scottish karting and motor racing community, past and present, for all the fun I've had, as well as all the help with this book. Thanks, in no particular order, to Allan McNish, Mark Gallagher, Brian Smith, David Cawthorne, Tom McLaren, Robert Logan, Duncan and Joyce Coulthard, Derek Butcher, Paul and Mark and Jackie Stewart, DC himself, and David Leslie junior, who is perhaps the most frank and honest racing driver I have ever encountered.

Thanks also to *Karting* magazine, *Motoring News*, and *The Scotsman*, whose archives, collectively, carefully chart the career of David Coulthard — and to David Hayhoe, author of *The Grand Prix Data Book*, for verifying statistics. Finally, thanks to Hugh Hunston with whom I shared the excitement of DC's early career, the horror of the first day of May 1994, and David's first few Grands Prix, until my once bitter rival decided to change careers and leave me to follow 'The boy', as we always called him, on my own.

The illustrations are from LAT Photographic except where stated otherwise.

• CHAPTER ONE •

The new boy makes his mark

'IF THAT WAS a classic pole position lap by Schumacher,' said David Coulthard after the first qualifying session for the 1995 San Marino Grand Prix, 'then I think we can beat it.' This was a royal 'we', it should be noted, and referred to himself and not to any joint efforts by Coulthard and his Williams Renault team-mate Damon Hill.

Although Hill had won the previous race in Argentina, after Coulthard's car broke down while he was leading, the Scot already *knew* he could beat Hill. In the same race, just the second of his first full season in Formula 1, and only his tenth Grand Prix, he had proved to himself — after a brilliant overtaking manoeuvre that must have shaken Schumacher's confidence somewhat — that he was also well up to beating the German in a straight fight.

From a driver who exactly one year before had been no more than another young hopeful with a Formula 1 testing contract in his pocket, this dismissal of the World Champion in just 17 words might seem like supreme arrogance. But as Coulthard — the most dynamic new talent to enter F1 in years — observed after scoring the first podium position of his career by finishing second to Hill in the 1994 Portuguese Grand Prix, winning is all about confidence. 'Most of Schumacher's results come from his confidence. That is what makes the difference between winning and losing at this level of the sport.'

Coulthard's confidence before the start of the San Marino Grand Prix had never been higher. Until Schumacher's Benetton Renault lapped the heavily revised Imola circuit in one minute 27.274 seconds, and until Gerhard Berger in the Ferrari in front of a home crowd in the last minute of qualifying took provisional second spot with 1.27.282, 24-year-old Coulthard, the newest kid on the block, had dominated practice.

It was always going to be a dramatic Grand Prix. San Marino 1995 was Formula 1 staring at itself in the mirror and wondering if it liked what it saw. In 1994 both Roland Ratzenberger and Ayrton Senna had been killed at the same event. When the Formula 1 circus arrived this year — charged with emotion, and crowded by media persons eager to record every tearstain, every commemorative bouquet — what the sport, and the fans, wanted more than anything else was a good, fast, exciting race in which no-one got hurt. The race, it turned out, was all those things. Better still, it was won by Senna's team-mate Damon Hill on whom such a heavy burden had fallen after the triple World Champion's death.

Schumacher stormed off into the lead on wet tyres on a drying track, Berger — home favourite on a circuit just a few miles away

The start of the dramatic 1995 San Marino Grand Prix (ICN UK Bureau).

from the Ferrari factory — was tracking him. Two seconds back sat David Coulthard, and behind him, showing no signs of wanting or indeed being able to force his way through, sat Damon Hill. Behind that, Jean Alesi in the second Ferrari. A long way back, in a completely different race, was Mika Hakkinen in sixth place and, somewhere beyond that, Nigel Mansell, the man who might have been at the wheel of Coulthard's car, a former World Champion making his long-awaited comeback to F1 in a McLaren Mercedes that had needed to be redesigned to accommodate his bulk.

Berger was first into the pits for the inevitable change to dry tyres and, within three laps, was the fastest man on the circuit by nearly two seconds a lap. Schumacher, racing a car that had been virtually rebuilt after a high-speed crash during second qualifying, angled the Benetton into the pits immediately after he heard the news on the pit-to-car radio, to fit dry tyres and take on fuel. Coulthard was now leading the race, the sixth he had led in his 11-race F1 career.

The sole team orders stated that the two team-mates must not take each other off

Some measure of the pressure on Schumacher comes from the fact that on his first flying lap with the new tyres he lost it, spun, spun again, hit the wall, spun, hit the wall again, and removed two wheels from the Benetton. Then there were only four drivers up front. Hill, who had also heard the news about Berger on dry tyres, was leaving the pits when Schumacher crashed. Coulthard was just coming in for what would turn out to be a slightly slower stop. When the race settled, two laps later, Berger led from Hill, Alesi climbing all over the rear of Coulthard in third place. This was what F1 was all about, what the fans had come to see.

When Berger came in for fuel on the 21st lap he stalled the engine, took vital seconds to restart and then there were three — Hill, Coulthard, and Alesi. For Hill in the lead, there was some comfort to be drawn from the fact that, although Coulthard was in his wheel tracks, the sole team order stated that the two team-mates must not take each other off. So while Coulthard was free to pass him, if he could, he must not force his way through and risk a crash.

Coulthard conducted a desperate but highly skilled defensive battle with Alesi (ICN UK Bureau).

Alesi, swarming all over the back of Coulthard's car, could, perhaps would, do anything he needed to get past. Alesi, driving the legendary number 27 Ferrari, the man who had catapulted to fame by, however briefly, passing Ayrton Senna in the Canadian Grand Prix five years before, had more than 80 races under his belt without a win. He was a desperate man in a marque desperate for a win, especially at home.

Coulthard, under tremendous pressure from Alesi — even occasionally banging wheels — tracked his team-mate, always looking for the way through, always trying to hold the Ferrari at bay as the three weaved through the backmarkers. But Coulthard was playing his own game. It was a game he had been playing since making his debut in kart racing at the age of 12.

On lap 25 Alesi pulled into the pits and Coulthard really piled on the pressure. Then, tucked just too closely under the leader's rear wing, he lost it, spun on the Villeneuve curve, quickly recovered and set off again after Hill. With his scheduled pit stop due any minute, the Scot went straight in for fuel and a change of tyres, his old ones covered in gravel. When he emerged, and leader Hill rejoined after his second stop, there were just seven seconds between them. Alesi, in the leading Ferrari, was another seven seconds behind.

In his anxiety for a fast stop, however, the young Scot had broken the 120 kph speed limit in the pit lane. An electronic speed limiter, one that the drivers can select to ensure that their cars remain below the 120 kph limit, was fitted to all cars after the previous year's Imola race following an incident when four mechanics were hurt. 'I had selected the limiter in first gear, then I changed into second to prevent wheelspin. Before I could engage the limiter in second gear I had broken the speed limit. I sort of hoped I might get away with it, but they caught me and called me in.'

He was called in for a 10-second stop/go penalty which helped cost him the race. The result would now be between Hill and Alesi. Coulthard apparently would have to settle for third place, with Berger a distant fourth. Unknown to the Scot, however, a kerb had

Right *Preparing for the 1995 season in Brazil where Coulthard's first run would be just two thousandths of a second behind Damon Hill in the first timed practice session.*

Left *Hmmm. Only third fastest in qualifying.*

damaged the endplate on the front wing of the Williams and when he was called in to have this replaced just 20 laps from the end, he lost nearly half a minute, letting Berger through into third.

And that, it turned out, was the story of the 1995 San Marino Grand Prix. The racing was fast, tempers were at times furious, no-one had been even slightly hurt, and F1 could look forward to the future with guarded optimism. Furthermore, the season promised genuine competition in store. No fewer than five drivers (Hill, Schumacher, Berger, Alesi and Coulthard) and three teams (Williams, Benetton and Ferrari) were in with a chance of the drivers' and constructors' titles. In 1994 there had been only three drivers (Senna, Schumacher and Hill) and two teams (Williams and Benetton). The two years before that, there had been only one driver (Prost in 1993, Mansell in 1992) and one team (Williams) with a realistic hope.

After the race Coulthard admitted, 'today I just made too many mistakes, first spinning, then speeding in the pits.' Jean Alesi — notoriously difficult to pass on the circuit, and a man whose utterings can be as fiery and undisciplined as his driving style — turned on the Scot with the sort of back-handed compliment that, from him, confirms that a new driver has really arrived in Formula 1. 'I have had good battles with lots of other drivers,' spat the French Sicilian after the race, 'but he is one of the most incorrect drivers I have ever seen.' Coulthard remained cool. 'I don't know what Alesi was complaining about. It was a good race. That is what racing is all about after all.'

Others have commented on Coulthard's desperate but highly skilled defensive battle with Alesi. Either way, there was no doubting that, like him or loathe him, the new kid on the block was determined, quick, and driving a fast car. Courageous too. Looking forward to the next race, in Spain, he said: 'I am very confident now because I am on the pace and I know so much more about Formula 1 than I did when I turned up for my first race there last year. Then I knew absolutely zero. If I had realised that then, I would have been a lot more nervous!'

Coulthard has been demonstrating his agility since the very start of the 1995 season in Brazil. Right from first practice.

On the Friday, in the first timed practice session for the Brazilian Grand Prix, Damon Hill took his Williams Renault round the 2.7 mile Interlagos circuit in one minute 21.664 seconds. It was the fastest time. Damon Hill was very definitely hot. Even as Hill backed off and relaxed on his slowing down lap, David Coulthard lapped the same circuit in one minute 21.666 seconds, just two thousandths of a second slower. Schumacher was third fastest — nearly a whole second a lap slower.

For Coulthard, just three days away from his 24th birthday, it was the latest confirmation that he had well and truly arrived in F1. It was also a warning, should his team-mate need one, that the much publicised power struggles between them the previous season were going to be a fact of life, however urbane relations might now seem to be, as expressed to the media. To put the lap into some sort of context, it was not only the first time Coulthard had ever driven on

Below *Yes, of course, Damon, I'll be the perfect number two driver to you this season.*

Right *The perfect number two driver . . . now, there's a funny thought.*

the South American continent, never mind the circuit, and it came after a week of suffering with tonsilitis which had prevented him completing the gruelling daily regime a Formula 1 driver needs to undergo just to be able to drive the car, never mind race it.

This first race of the new season was always going to be sensational. The circuit is near Sao Paulo, Ayrton Senna's home town. Emotions ran high for the Brazilians, still openly mourning the loss of their national hero, whose death had given the young Williams test driver his opening as an F1 racing driver.

In Friday's first official practice session Damon Hill, perhaps not surprisingly, set fastest time with a lap of one minute 20.081 seconds. Second fastest — albeit nearly a second adrift — was Gerhard Berger, again not surprisingly knowing both his skill and Ferrari's history of doing well whenever there is an engine capacity change (this year from 3.5 litres to 3 litres) in Formula 1. Coulthard, struggling with massive understeer, was three-tenths of a second behind the Austrian, but still nearly one second a lap faster than Michael Schumacher.

The World Champion, going into one of the fastest corners of his fastest lap, suffered a steering failure which he would subsequently blame on the bumpiness of the circuit. Despite having been

Of course there's a lot of glamour in Brazil. But what will Andrea say, never mind my mum?

No fewer than six British drivers lined up at the first race of the 1995 season. Coulthard is pictured with (from left) Mark Blundell standing in for Nigel Mansell in the McLaren; Martin Brundle (who didn't actually drive in that race); Eddie Irvine, Jordan; Johnny Herbert, Benetton; and Damon Hill.

completely resurfaced since the last Grand Prix the track was so bad that even Rubens Barrichello, the new local hero, called for it to be ripped up and relaid before the 1996 race.

The terror of a steering failure in a racing car cannot be over-emphasized, not least because that is believed to have been the reason behind Ayrton Senna's fatal crash. If the brakes fail at speed the driver can use the steering and throttle to spin the car to a halt. If a tyre blows the driver retains control over throttle, steering and brakes. If the throttle sticks open he can use the engine cut-out, brakes and steering to bring the car to a halt. If the steering goes the driver becomes a helpless passenger in an unguided missile.

Schumacher was lucky. After the car halted he jumped out, leapt on to a tyre barrier — and pondered just what the hell was going on. Later, he told his team in no uncertain terms that either the problem was fixed, or he was out of Sunday's race. Schumacher's mechanics worked until 5 am the next day to fix the steering. Schumacher

Second place in Brazil was overshadowed by a fuel row which saw Coulthard and Michael Schumacher (the winner) disqualified. But at this stage Schumacher, Coulthard, and Gerhard Berger look fairly cheerful (ICN UK Bureau).

would, of course, race.

In the second qualifying session on Saturday afternoon Schumacher crashed again, but not until he had set second fastest time of the day behind Damon Hill. Hill had not improved on his Friday time but Schumacher did, so did Coulthard. So too did Johnny Herbert in the second Benetton. The Ferraris were fifth and sixth.

In the early morning warm-up on race day, Coulthard was fastest. In the chronology of a Grand Prix, which begins with the first untimed session on the Friday and continues until the chequered flag has dropped, this can sometimes be significant, sometimes not. In theory at least, warm-up is the first time the drivers run the cars in race trim set-up for two reliable hours rather than four laps of speed. Sometimes, however, it is no more than another chance to psyche the opposition by heading the all-important time sheets. The time sheets, issued after every time the cars go out on race weekend, analyse their performance to one thousandth of a second, only one thousandth of one kilometre per hour. Top of the sheets is the only place to be — and where Coulthard was on race day morning in Brazil.

As the cars lined up on the grid on Sunday afternoon, with every-one hoping this opening race would herald the start of a happier, less controversial season, it seemed that Formula 1 was still not free of the swarm of technical troubles that had plagued the sport last year. A fuel sample supplied by Elf for the Renault engines of both Williams and Benetton had failed pre-race scrutineering in Brazil despite having passed scrutiny in Europe by the FIA, the sport's governing body. The results of the race would therefore only be provisional for any drivers with Renault engines who finished. Some drivers were informed of the situation by their team before the start. David Coulthard was not.

But as the 26 Formula 1 cars lined up on the dummy grid, the biggest thing on most drivers' minds was surviving the first corner which, whether you are a 12-year-old kart racer or a 42-year-old Formula 1 veteran, is always the most dangerous moment of your life. They all survived, Schumacher outdragging Hill to the first corner, Coulthard slotting in behind his team-mate, Herbert getting lost, Hakkinen flying, Alesi out-accelerating Berger, then Irvine, Katayama and Salo in less than the blink of an eye.

Within a couple of laps it became obvious there were only three cars in the race, Schumacher and Hill, then Coulthard stalking, a

The first Grand Prix in Argentina for 14 years was a nightmare in the wet. Coulthard took provisional pole.

couple of seconds back but pulling away from Hakkinen, watching, waiting for a mistake from the front two. On lap four Hill attacked Schumacher, nearly got through, was forced to back off and, in the scrabbling, off-line recovery nearly lost second place as Coulthard pounced, drew alongside and nearly, *nearly* got past. But it was too early for such a risk. Next lap order, Schumacher, Hill, then Coulthard, then, after a bigger gap, Hakkinen, then the rest.

That was the pattern for the early part of the race. Hill harrying Schumacher, Coulthard five seconds back. 'I could not keep up their pace so I backed off and decided to run at a comfortable lap time,' he said. The three of them were all the time pulling away from Hakkinen and the rest. Gerhard Berger was a distant fifth, not that it seemed to matter.

> *Coulthard, who had arrived beaming,*
> *looked as if someone had punched him*

Schumacher came in early on lap 18 for the first of what was obviously going to be three pit stops. For four laps Hill led before coming in for his first stop followed, one lap later, by the Scot. The Williams Renault pair favoured a two-stop strategy. Hill came out fast, ahead of Schumacher, and that seemed to be it on a track where there are very few passing opportunities. Then, on lap 20, Hill had trouble with the automatic gearbox. On the next lap he had serious trouble changing down and the car spun. The transmission troubles and bad luck which had dogged Coulthard's 1994 season from his very first race, and which had denied him at least one victory, were suddenly Hill's troubles.

Now it was a two-car race, Coulthard tracking Schumacher. The rest, still led by Hakkinen, were more than half a minute back and drifting away. On lap 35 Schumacher pulled in for his second stop. Coulthard took the lead and started to try to tease out enough of a gap to let him make his second stop and emerge close enough behind Schumacher to guarantee he would be first when the German exited the pits for the third time. But it was not to be. Even with only a dozen survivors, and both Schumacher and Coulthard lapping everyone else on the circuit, the Brazilian Grand Prix came down, quite simply, to traffic. Gerhard Berger, who was to finish third, a whole lap behind, appeared to be very helpful when Schumacher came up to lap him. When Coulthard arrived, he appeared less so.

After the race, after the national anthems and the flag waving and the champagne spraying, the three drivers arrived in the press room for the post-race interview which is broadcast all over the world. But as they took their places in front of the media and began the other post-race ritual of downing large quantities of mineral water, Bob Constanduros, who traditionally fronts these interviews, congratulated the drivers — but added the bombshell that the results were only provisional in view of a possible irregularity with the fuel of the Benetton number 1 and Williams number 6 cars.

Schumacher, upon whose face one can normally read every emotion, appeared indifferent. Coulthard, who had arrived beaming, looked as though someone had punched him somewhere very precious. Gerhard Berger, ever the joker, was delighted. 'No, no, the protest stands, they are disqualified.' Everyone except Schumacher and Coulthard laughed. Good old Berger.

The fuel samples supplied by Elf, and approved by the FIA in Europe were not, according to officials at the track, legal. The thought of Elf, oldest continuous fuel supplier in F1, cheating seemed simply out of the question. The thought of the FIA bungling, again, did not. Schumacher and Coulthard were for the moment disqualified. The outcome of a vigorous appeal by both Benetton and Williams would have to wait until after the Argentinian Grand Prix two weeks later. Coulthard, who had not been warned of potential problems with the fuel before the start of the race, was livid. 'They should,' he said quietly, 'have told me.'

The mental and physical build up to the 1995 Argentinian Grand Prix, first in that country for 14 years, began just three hours after the end of the Brazilian race with the madcap escape from the circuit. No-one, save possibly Brazilian drivers, can stand the Brazilian Grand Prix, especially in Sao Paulo.

It is a rough, tough, nasty place where, unless you are one of the handful of super rich, you could not possibly want to live. Visitors, most of whom are drawn by the Grand Prix, want nothing more than to get through the journeys from the airport to the track to the airport and the days in between, and hope that their car does not

Main picture *Put your light on the marshal advised, as if it mattered. No-one would get near Coulthard as he confirmed his pole position in the second session, even as the heavens opened again.*

Inset *One of the fruits of success in Formula 1, pole position in the pole position press conference. 'Well,' says Coulthard for the first time, 'it happened like this . . .'*

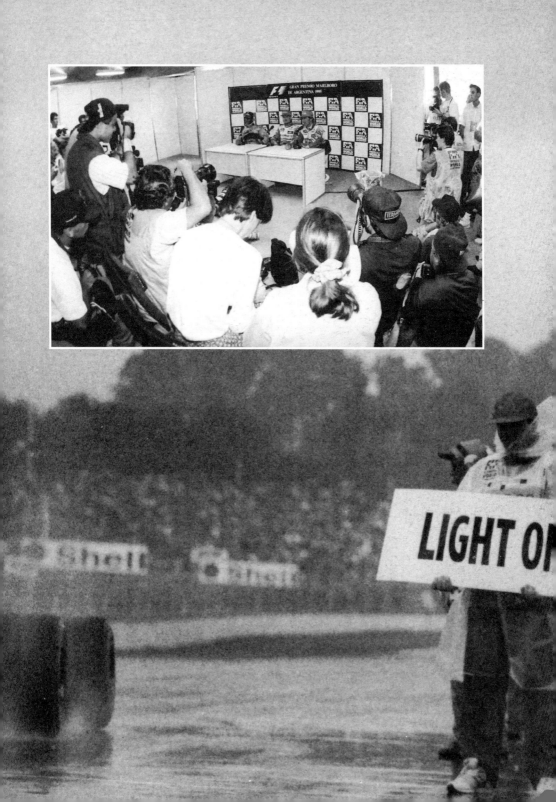

break down. If they are on their own, and their car does break down, they hope that the end comes quickly. Bob Constanduros puts it succinctly. 'If you survive Sao Paulo, if your hire car keeps going, if your hotel is OK, if your communications work, if you get your story across, all without trouble, then you know that the rest of the year is going to be a good one.'

The fastest way out of Sao Paulo after the race is on the 9.30 pm British Airways flight to London Heathrow. You leave Brazil in the middle of the night and arrive in London around noon. The difference between the two countries, even to experienced travellers, is as obvious as night and day. At the airport, queuing to get on the plane, Coulthard looks pleased with himself, despite the fuel row.

'What about the World Championship?' I ask him.

'I don't want to think about the World Championship until I have won a Grand Prix,' he replies.

But the idea had obviously occurred to him, the very audacity of the thought that he could have a serious go at winning the World Championship in his first full season of Formula 1 (and if so of challenging Emerson Fittipaldi's record as youngest World Champion, winning the title in 1972 aged 25 years, eight months).

In only his tenth F1 race he had achieved pole position

A fortnight later, in the pouring wet of the first practice for the Argentinian Grand Prix, David Coulthard grabbed provisional pole with a lap more than one second faster than his team-mate Damon Hill could manage. Third fastest was Schumacher, two-tenths of a second behind Hill. On the Saturday, in the final qualifying session in which most drivers waited until the final 10 minutes before venturing out on to the drying track, Damon Hill came back with two fast laps on the trot, either of them, he thought, good enough to guarantee him pole position for the race.

As he eased his Williams into the pit lane garage at the end of his stint, Hill sat back to watch the results of his rivals on the small monitor the mechanics placed on the bodywork in front of his face. Above it, he could see the rain starting to fall on the other side of the

Inset *Race day, a dry track and 'Do I feel lucky?'*

Main picture *Though he led from pole in both starts in Argentina, and twice seemed certain to run away with his first victory, Coulthard lasted just 16 laps before his car failed — for the second time. After the first time he got going again, caught and eventually passed the World Champion (ICN UK Bureau).*

Hill tried to hang on after being passed in the pits, but as it turned out he didn't have to worry.

track, ready to obliterate the marginally dry line which had given him his time. With just seconds remaining in the final qualifying session, Coulthard bullied and cajoled his sliding, slithering Williams car round the Argentinian circuit eight-tenths of a second faster than his team-mate. He had won the first pole position start of his Formula 1 career. Almost unnoticed, Michael Schumacher performed similar heroics to cement third place on the starting grid.

On the Sunday morning warm-up, on the first dry track of the weekend, Coulthard was a disappointing fifth fastest behind Hill, Berger, Alesi, and Schumacher. If he was at all worried, it did not show. He had, after all, been fastest in the warm-up in Brazil — for all the good it had done him.

As Coulthard led the parade lap of a Grand Prix for the first time in his life, and in only his tenth appearance, the pressure must have felt immense. With Damon Hill starting alongside him, the World Champion immediately behind, Eddie Irvine alongside him and another 22 ambitious drivers lined up behind them, the risk of making a mistake at the start seemed extremely high.

Coulthard made a perfect start. Hill slotted in behind, Schumacher behind that. Beyond them the grid had gone mad. Jean Alesi, fighting for his career, skidded and felt his Ferrari tapped from behind going into the first corner. In the resulting chaos five cars were destroyed. The race was red-flagged to a halt at the end of the opening lap. Four drivers — Alesi, Hakkinen, Barrichello and Herbert — grabbed their custom-made seats from their cars and rushed back to the pits. They knew that the spare cars were awaiting them. Barrichello, dramatically shorter than team-mate Eddie Irvine, for whom the spare car had been set up, would not quite make his grid position for the second start. He started from the back of the grid. The fifth driver, Bertrand Gachot in a Pacific, had no spare car.

The second start to the first Argentinian Grand Prix in 14 years simply doubled the pressure on Coulthard who, like every pole position man before him, had to summon every ounce of his concentration and willpower not to lose the crucially important advantage so hard won in qualifying.

Coulthard made no mistake. Hill, his car hesitating for just a fraction of a second, did. When the cars crossed the line at the end of the

The President of Argentina presents the pole position trophy to David Coulthard (ICN UK Bureau).

first lap Coulthard was two seconds clear of Schumacher. Hill was swarming all over the German's gearbox. Six laps into the race and Coulthard was driving away, now four seconds clear with Hill still swarming fruitlessly over the Benetton. Then, on lap six, as he cleared the first hairpin after the finishing straight, the electrics on Coulthard's car suddenly died.

The Scot coasted round the corner losing vital seconds. But, just as the Schumacher-Hill combination appeared in his mirrors, the Williams Renault came back to life. Coulthard, finding the car suddenly alive and in first gear, left long thick strips of rubber on the tarmac as he sought to get back up to speed. But Schumacher and Hill were through. He was down to third. Three laps later there were three cars contesting the lead — Schumacher, Hill, Coulthard — passing as fast as you could say their names. On the next lap Hill ducked inside Schumacher and was gone. Coulthard, desperate to catch his team-mate, first had to pass the World Champion. After the Brazilian Grand Prix he had told me, 'sure, Michael is quick, but he can be beaten'.

On the fourteenth lap Coulthard was tucked right up under Schumacher's rear wing as he completed the lap, his car sliding all over the road as he traded downforce for closeness. Ahead of Schumacher, just two car lengths away, was the Minardi Ford of Pierluigi Martini.

On to the start-finish straight and as Schumacher slipstreamed the Minardi ready to take Martini at the end of the straight Coulthard, coming like a train, ducked right. Schumacher moved right to block him. Coulthard, travelling slightly faster, ducked left and drew alongside. Schumacher, on the inside line, might still win the corner. Then the Scot stayed off the brakes longer, twisted his car to the right, in front of Schumacher and inside the Minardi and, in one of the best overtaking manoeuvres seen in F1 for years, he was in front of Martini and Schumacher was behind. For Coulthard, it was the chance to go hunting for Hill, now 10 seconds in front. For Schumacher it was perhaps the most devastating blow to his confidence he had experienced in Formula 1.

Right *Coulthard and his business manager Tim Wright shake hands on yet another lucrative deal and he is still only two races into his first full F1 season.*

30

On lap 16 Hill pitted, took a leisurely 15.5 seconds, and emerged in third place. Coulthard, all het up, really lit the fires. He started to pull away. He lasted just two more laps. On the first corner after starting his seventeenth lap, the electrics died. The Williams rolled off the track and on to the grass.

After parking the car, and watching Schumacher retake the lead, the Scot sat for long, long seconds reflecting on his luck. In the adrenalin high from which his body would take hours to recover, it is doubtful if he would have been able to sit and reason it out beyond the abysmal disappointment of not finishing another race. Yet everyone who had watched the race knew the truth. The 1995 World Championship was now at least a three-horse race.

By the time Damon Hill crossed the line to take his tenth F1 victory nearly one and a half hours later, Jean Alesi had confirmed that Ferrari were back in the hunt, and Gerhard Berger led the title race with 11 points to Damon Hill's 10. Michael Schumacher, nearly half a minute behind Hill, had the appearance of a broken man.

The post-fuel row Brazilian results at that stage still stood. It was not until the following week that the FIA decided to overturn the disqualification of Schumacher and Coulthard, reinstating them as winner and runner-up respectively of the Brazilian Grand Prix. The drivers had their points restored, moving the German into the lead in the Drivers' Championship with 14 points, ahead of Damon Hill with 10 points, Jean Alesi with eight, and David Coulthard fourth with six points. However the Constructors' points were not restored to the Benetton and Williams teams, whose punishment also included a hefty fine.

A poignant postscript to the Argentinian Grand Prix. Coulthard received the first Carlitos Menem Memorial Trophy, now presented to the pole position winner each year in memory of the only son of the Argentine President. The 26-year-old rally driver was killed in a helicopter crash a month before the GP when travelling to a competition.

• CHAPTER TWO •

Scotland's Young Pretender

'I'M OBVIOUSLY NOT some hairy-arsed Highlander,' said David Coulthard, age 23, occupation, Formula 1 racing driver. 'But I am immensely proud to be Scottish.'

With these words, shortly after finishing second in the 1994 Portuguese Grand Prix at Estoril driving for the Williams Renault team, David Coulthard both embraced his past and reached out to grasp what promised to be a glittering future. He was tacitly adopting the mantle of Young Pretender, the one who would attempt to follow two of the greatest Formula 1 drivers the world has ever known, hoping to take up where they left off.

Scotland has an impressive racing heritage. In the 45 years of modern Formula 1, Britain has sired no fewer than seven World Champions who have between them accounted for 11 World Championship titles. Two of the seven came from Scotland, Jim Clark and Jackie Stewart. They won five of the 11 world titles — Clark in 1963 and 1965, and Stewart in 1969, 1971 and 1973. This is a towering achievement from a country — and everyone in Scotland regards it as a country, no matter that it is ruled from London — with a population one-tenth that of England.

In a sport where every move of every car and driver, wherever it happens to be in the world, is timed to one thousandth of a second,

Left *Before the 1994 Portuguese GP Coulthard had wondered if he could shrug off the run of bad luck that had cost him at least two podium finishes.*

statistics come thick and fast and, if you let them, can easily overwhelm the senses. But consider these. The two Scottish champions between them scored 52 Grand Prix wins, the five English champions just 64.

Including Coulthard's results up to the start of the 1995 season, the Scots scored 51 pole positions compared with 71 achieved by English drivers, and 45 fastest laps compared with 65.

He watched TV wearing a helmet to build up his neck muscles

Jim Clark's batting average, the number of wins compared with the number of Grand Prix starts, is still a record at over one in three — 25 victories from 72 starts. His 33 pole positions remained a record for more than two decades until beaten by Ayrton Senna, and the 25 Grand Prix wins were bested by Stewart, who scored his 27th GP win in 1973, five years after Clark's death. Stewart's record, in turn, stood for 14 years until Alain Prost finally beat it in 1987. Quite an example for ambitious young Coulthard to follow.

There is another element that makes the statistics all the more remarkable. Save for the 1986 season of Johnny Dumfries, driving for Lotus and playing second fiddle to a talent as huge as Ayrton Senna's, Scotland has been without a representative in Formula 1 for over two decades until David Coulthard took part in the 1994 Spanish Grand Prix.

Coulthard cannot remember when exactly he decided he wanted to become a Grand Prix driver, but his mother Joyce recalls his rigorous training regime which began at a fairly early age. Aware that the forces acting on a driver were becoming increasingly harsh, largely through the effects of aerodynamics, the teenage Coulthard used to watch television lying on his side wearing a crash helmet. Every 15 minutes or so he would turn over and lie on the other side — to build up his neck and shoulder muscles.

Son of a frustrated would-be Formula 1 driver, Coulthard was

Main picture *You're not getting me out of here, no way. I don't care if Nigel Mansell did send you (ICN UK Bureau).*

Inset *After the Portuguese GP, with winner Hill and third placed Mika Hakkinen on the podium, he felt good.*

raised with a veneration for Scotland's motorsport heroes. Jim Clark was killed almost exactly three years before David Coulthard was born; and when Jackie Stewart retired, David was little more than a toddler. But the influence of both drivers has been undeniable. Although Stewart was to play a key role in his graduation towards Formula 1, it was Clark whom David idolised. When he finished fifth in Canada in only his second race he was immensely proud of the fact that his achievement had exactly matched that of Clark, who finished fifth in his own second F1 race, the 1960 Belgian Grand Prix.

Quite why such a tiny nation as Scotland has had such an impact at the highest level of motorsport has no easy answer. Perhaps Jackie Stewart was closest when he once talked of being driven by a deep-seated insecurity shared by both himself and Clark. Clark for example is remembered for his fingernails which were bitten down to the quick and, out of a racing car, for his complete inability to make up his mind or reach a decision.

There is a place for this apparent 'insecurity' however. Stewart says: 'If you are convinced mentally about your own superiority you

The following year, DC would be back at Estoril testing, taking the FW17 out as a full-time Formula 1 driver (The Scotsman).

Above left *Jackie Stewart, three times World Champion, and later to become Coulthard's mentor, in the days when fellow Scots knew him as Hairy Head.* (The Scotsman).

Above right *Jim Clark (right) and Graham Hill before the start of the 1966 RAC Rally of Great Britain. The following season they were F1 partners at Lotus — the last pairing of two British drivers in a team until Coulthard joined Graham's son Damon at Williams* (The Scotsman).

are disregarding the most serious threat, namely the competitive element of your adversary. If you are so dogmatic as to believe in yourself to that extent, you clearly do not respect the level of the competition. I would far rather put my opposition up on a pedestal and be satisfied when I have shot at them successfully.

'It has no benefit at all for you to have a false impression of your own talent. You can kid a lot of people, but you can't kid yourself.

'People turn around to me and say, "Jackie, you've been successful". And that is true, up to a point. But am I as successful as I could have been? I'm really not sure. I think I could have done a lot better. Being successful is one thing, but reaching your true, ultimate potential, is entirely another.'

To some, perhaps those whose lives revolve round the hype and egotistical circus of Formula 1, his words may sound oddly self-doubt-

Left *The Young Pretender met the Old Master when David signed up with Paul Stewart Racing in 1990.*

ing. To others — particularly Scots who, almost by tradition, have an innate loathing of the pompous and the arrogant — they mean no more than the simple expression of down-to-earth values and commonsense.

Robert Burns, probably the most famous Scot in history — as opposed to Jackie Stewart who is the most famous living Scotsman — was renowned for his earthy philosophy. It is a philosophy that David Coulthard also embraces: big enough to battle with motorsport's best, yet humble enough to do the washing up at the kitchen sink.

The former Williams test driver, promoted to race driver after Senna's death in May 1994, says: 'I remember turning up in Spain and absolutely crapping myself because I had not driven the FW16 which was this year's car. I had only tested at Jerez and Estoril. I was nervous about how I would perform. That is all I ever get nervous about.

'Of course I am aware of the dangers, all the usual things you hear about. I am a nervous person away from the circuit because I fear not being able to perform, not being able to be quick and not having the potential to win — that's what I fear.'

Coulthard's father Duncan, whose personal involvement has been a feature throughout this success story, was never in any doubt that his son would perform. Indeed so convinced was he that David would become one of the F1 greats that he has retained every racing kart and racing car, every racing suit and crash helmet ever used by the lad including, it is believed, a 1994 Williams Renault FW16 replica prepared by the team for motor shows and exhibitions.

Whether David Coulthard would in fact live up to the performances of his illustrious countrymen, and prove his proud father right, remained to be seen. But the signs did look good.

CHAPTER THREE

A small village with big ambitions

TWYNHOLM, KIRKCUDBRIGHTSHIRE, population 280, is a typical Scottish hamlet — a handful of streets, a pub, a hotel and a couple of shops. Directly across the road from the village pub is a large, ugly shed-cum-garage which looks as if it had been reclaimed as World War 2 booty, transported to this unlikely site, and hand-built by locals looking to the future and all thinking furiously of the possibility one day, perhaps, of a job.

Tack-welded onto the front of this orange/red relic, in iron letters a metre high, are the words Hayton Coulthard. It is the trademark of one of Scotland's oldest road hauliers. The company was started here, around the turn of the century, by David Coulthard's great-grandfather and a partner called Hayton who was long ago bought out. It was continued by his grandfather, has been expanded by his father Duncan and will, no doubt, be tended by David's older brother, also Duncan.

The business thrives in a village so small that the inhabitants, according to typical Scottish wit, cannot even afford a village idiot, they have to take it in turns. It survives partly because of the intensive care of generations of Coulthards but also, one suspects, because — within a stone's throw of the Solway Firth — it is on the A75 Euroroute to the ferry port of Stranraer which is the UK's, and

This picture graced the cover of the February 1994 programme at Summerlee (The West of Scotland Kart Club).

This is how it all began. DC with father Duncan at his first race (Bob Geddes, Galloway News).

Europe's, gateway to Ireland. Duncan Coulthard senior is the man who supplies much of the economic wealth of this typical west Borders village set in a tiny valley between rolling hills. He is also a frustrated racing driver. He is, without doubt, the most frustrated racing driver in the history of Twynholm.

He makes no bones about this, and it is easy to understand why.

Duncan dallied with kart racing but never realised his dream, to drive in F1

Innes Ireland, the first Scot ever to win a Grand Prix when he gave Team Lotus its maiden F1 victory in the 1961 US Grand Prix, was the son of the Coulthards' local vet. Jim Clark, another Borders man — though from the eastern end of the border separating Scotland from England — was the dominant force in Formula 1 when Duncan was at the age when he most wanted to be a Formula 1 driver but had, instead, to look after the haulage company. This was at the height of the swinging sixties when a whole generation believed that, one day soon, they could change the whole world. And while the Beatles sang *All you need is love*, and the Coulthards struggled with the business and planned their family, Jackie Stewart picked up the mantle of his countryman Clark and won three World Championships.

Duncan briefly dallied with kart racing locally. But the demands of the business, which was not in the best of health when he inherited it, met his future wife Joyce at a dance in a local village hall, and began to raise a family, meant that he could never realise his ultimate dream, to drive in a Formula 1 race.

By the time that Duncan junior, David and his sister Linsey had begun to grow up, however, the company was on a sound financial footing and Duncan and Joyce could enjoy their children, counsel them and, maybe, to guide them a little. And, Duncan may have reasoned, if one of them wants to become a racing driver, then who am I to stand in the way? More important, perhaps crucial in a sport that costs a king's ransom just to begin to compete, the Coulthards could, by now, afford it.

Duncan Coulthard would be mortally offended if anyone described the family as rich. But they are, undeniably, prosperous. Comfortably

Duncan Coulthard with Brian Smith, the karter who painted the now famous Saltire on DC's helmet (Wigtown Free Press).

Jim Clark, first Scottish World Champion and Coulthard's first motorsport hero (The Scotsman).

enough off, for instance, to be able to afford 'his and hers' Mercedes-Benz cars, a big house with a swimming pool, a paddock for the kids to play in. Comfortable enough to afford a small twin-engine plane in which Duncan is flown all over the UK visiting the blue chip clients with whom he does business. Duncan, 52, is a typical self-made Scot. A man unashamedly proud of the fact that while now mixing with captains of industry, he can still get his hands dirty fixing a diesel engine or have a drink in the pub with the lads. After receiving David's telephone call about getting the Williams drive in the 1994 Spanish Grand Prix, he rushed down to the pub to tell everyone. And you can be sure that since that great day Twynholm folk have become F1 experts, following their young neighbour's career with personal pride.

They were urged to enjoy life and make best use of themselves

Duncan likes to think of himself as a boss who can be hard and uncompromising at work yet as couthy (a Scots word meaning, loosely, down-to-earth) as they come in the rest of his life. Compared with her big, rough, tough and capable husband, Joyce looks to the casual observer like a mere slip of a Scottish lass — petite, slender, almost frail. Yet to describe Joyce Coulthard as frail would be about as accurate as to describe her son's performance on the race track as brisk. Joyce is a fiercely proud mum who would go to any lengths to defend her children. At the same time, she would go even further to ensure that they not only enjoyed life to the full but, perhaps more important, made the best of themselves while doing so.

While Duncan senior flits around the country maintaining eye contact with customers as he nurtures the family firm, Joyce keeps open house and provides, in the Scottish tradition, a warm welcome for all the friends that the Coulthard children bring home. David Cawthorne — now working at Lloyds insuring athletes and celebrities — was a school friend of David Coulthard, and shared a home with him in Chiswick and, before that, Milton Keynes. He still regards the Coulthard household as a second home. 'What?' he exclaims when you say you have been anywhere near Twynholm.

'You mean you didn't go in to see Joyce?' To him, that is unthinkable.

For Duncan, only too happy to let his children enjoy all the things he never had the time — or perhaps money — for as a youngster, it was relatively easy to give them their head. David Coulthard's first taste of the speed and power of the internal combustion engine came in the family paddock where he and his big brother played with motorcycles their father had thoughtfully provided. Just on the offchance, you understand.

To Joyce those early years must have been sheer hell. It was she who had to pick up the pieces when, as adventurous children always will, the boys came home with bruises, cuts, scratches and even the occasional broken or dislocated limb. She still recalls the pair of them side by side in the lounge with their arms in plaster, each one in a deck chair because that was the most comfortable seating. Her reward — one of her rewards — came on the day when David made his Formula 1 debut in the Williams Renault at the 1994 Spanish Grand Prix. Duncan was so proud that he could barely speak. Joyce was so proud she could barely restrain herself. Overhearing two bystanders pondering the identity of the new Williams Renault driver from the viewpoint of the opulent Paddock Club suite high above the pits, she was not backwards about going forward. 'You know who that is,' she said. 'That's my David, my boy!'

Clark in action behind the wheel of his Lotus 25 — so relaxed that he could afford to pose for photographer friends (Graham Gauld).

Given the Coulthards' financial circumstances provided by Duncan's labours, and the strong family bonds forged by Joyce, it is virtually impossible to think of two more perfect parents for a budding Formula 1 driver. They have always been supportive, of the sport as well as their offspring. When local kart racing fans — tired of travelling at least 60 miles to the nearest circuit at Larkhall — raised the money for their own track near his home, Duncan was ready and willing to enter the spirit of things, albeit at once removed, by sponsoring a local driver, Brian Smith. For Duncan, a shade too old to race, it was a way of keeping in touch with the scene and enjoying the vicarious thrill of nearly competing.

When David turned 12 years old the Coulthard family, especially Duncan, was rather delighted when he decided that he might like to try kart racing. Smith — who achieved some kind of racing immortality by first painting the distinctive Saltire pattern on DC's helmet — prepared Coulthard's karts for many of his early races. He recalls that it was an empty crisp packet and a fist-size stone which helped teach young David the braking techniques which he still uses to this day.

'It was his first time at Larkhall, and he just could not get his braking point for the right-hand corner at the end of the straight. He would either brake too early and make a mess of the corner, or brake too late and spin off. In the end I got an old crisp packet, laid it on the outside of the track at the braking point, and put a stone on it to hold it down. David showed complete faith and braked at the crisp packet and that was the problem solved.'

Smith remembers Allan McNish as the star of Scottish kart racing at that time. But Coulthard's ability soon became apparent. 'I used to watch David racing in the wet, and the control was unbelievable.'

Even in those days he was fastidious about maintaining his kart and keeping it clean. 'He used to spend hours cleaning and polishing it. Everything had to be just so, though he did not really know much about the mechanical side of things. That came later when he met the Leslie family in Formula Ford. Indeed it was amazing what the Leslies taught him in a very short time. He was very dedicated. We all shared this old caravanette, and after a Saturday spent

Right *Nattily dressed Innes Ireland, the first Scot to win a Grand Prix — his father was the Coulthard family's local vet* (The Scotsman).

testing we all wanted to sit up and have a few beers, but David used to keep on at us to have an early night so we would be up fresh next morning!'

The racing accident which gave Brian Smith the spare time to paint Coulthard's helmet — something to do while in hospital with a spine injury — also ended his own racing career. But the nerves which every driver experiences did not go away when he watched his young protege racing. 'I thought the greatest day of my life was when I won the Scottish championship. But when David won his first national title it was even worse. I was a nervous wreck and kept wondering if I had aligned the chain properly or bolted the engine on right. In fact I still have the engraved piston from the engine that David used to win, as a memento.'

David and his father always believed he would get to the top — 'we just knew'

Fast forward now to Sunday, 5 February 1995 and it is a driech day at Summerlee race track, Scotland's premier kart racing venue near Larkhall on the outskirts of Glasgow. (Driech is a peculiarly Scottish word which means, variously, cold, wet, windy — but above all, depressing. Some say the word sums up the Scottish climate. Meteorologists can provide much evidence to the contrary, but driech is the way everyone remembers it.) Once little more than a distorted kidney-shape track less than a quarter of a mile in length, Summerlee is now a world class kart circuit built, and funded, largely by enthusiastic members of the West of Scotland Kart Club. In the often bizarre but always close-knit ways of the Scottish karting fraternity its reconstruction was personally underwritten by a local judge and enthusiastic kart racer. This gentleman wore a genuine pith helmet in the pits.

Just under half a mile long, Summerlee offers a choice of two circuits. There is a relatively fast open track for the extremely rapid karts fitted with gearboxes, and an equally long, but more intricate circuit for the vast majority who use class one, non-gearbox karts. Non-gearbox karts dominate the paddock. Fathers and sons — and occasionally daughters — huddle round the racing machines which sit on raised stands under umbrellas, tents, caravan awnings and, sometimes, the sky. Beside each kart is a car or van containing the rest of the family, the vehicles' engines all ticking over quietly, heaters turned to full blast to get rid of condensation and provide some welcome warmth.

The first race meeting of the new year is particularly driech but, for the fathers at least, relieved a little by the wee dram of whisky with which Scots welcome the new year — sometimes well into February. In the paddock, perhaps a quarter of those who have turned up are there for the first time, the fathers prepared to spend what it takes; the youngsters, some barely eight years old, ready to do what is required.

Larkhall, or a track like it anywhere in the world, on a driech February day, is where motor racing all begins. Whether they admit it or not, every father and every competitor here at Summerlee shares but one dream, to make it to the very top, *to make it to Formula 1.* David Coulthard and his father always believed he would get to the top, even when things were difficult. 'We just knew.' Joyce's own personal philosophy will have eased any moments there may have been of self doubt. 'What is for you won't go by you,' she says.

At Summerlee they all know the odds. At the first race of the new

Ireland, who had a historic victory in the 1961 US Grand Prix, wins the 1962 Crystal Palace Trophy Race in a Lotus BRM (The Scotsman).

season, it is 12 to one for the beginners. Great odds, perhaps, until you consider that only one kart driver makes it into Formula 1 every dozen years or so. Even odds of 144 to one do not sound too bad, considering the potential rewards, until you consider that the same scene is being enacted at hundreds of circuits around the world. But this year, for the first time in the history of the track, and the first time in the history of Scottish karting, the New Year race meeting is extra special. Because someone *has* finally made it into the bigtime.

It is almost exactly 12 years since David Coulthard turned up with his father on a driech day at Summerlee. Some of the children now getting ready to race were not even born when David Coulthard made his karting debut at the age of 12. But the links with the past are very real. Wander round the paddock and you will meet a number of karters who raced against him but, for various reasons, stayed racing karts. Karting is a branch of motorsport all of its own.

In a corner near the clubhouse a guy called Dave Boyce has set up a stall selling wheels, pistons, tyres and oil — the high tech consumables of the sport. Boyce remains one of David Coulthard's closest friends and the man who, even today, lends the Williams Renault driver a kart so that the two can work out for the hell of it on quiet days at Summerlee. If they are lucky, those in the paddock know they might even meet DC (as he is most commonly nicknamed), for the Scottish karters are a close-knit clan and this is where they often meet.

Over here is Derek Butcher. A former champion on two wheels and four, Butcher owns Knockhill in Fife, Scotland's only dedicated racing circuit, the place where DC first drove a racing car. Today, Derek Butcher is just another ambitious father. Over there is David Leslie junior, Honda works driver in the 1995 British Touring Car Championship (BTCC), veteran of Le Mans and the World Sportscar Championship with Ecurie Ecosse. Leslie probably won more kart races at the old Summerlee than anyone else. He once, though few people know it, out-qualified Ayrton Senna in Formula 3. It was Leslie and his father, also called David, who first put DC in a racing car.

Right *Knockhill, November 1994. Six years after he drove his first race car at this circuit, David is negotiating with F1 giants Williams and McLaren* (The Scotsman).

John Cleland, former BTCC champion and leader of the 1995 Vauxhall works team, is today another ambitious father. So is Hugh McCaig, patron of Ecurie Ecosse, now BTCC challengers. But he is also a kart racing driver himself. And who's this wee guy who looks immensely fit? Allan McNish, once master of Larkhall, is currently development driver on the Lola Formula 1 project when he's not contesting the International Formula 3000 Championship in the Paul Stewart Racing team. Paul Stewart? Son of Jackie, of course.

The basic skills needed to race a kart successfully round Summerlee are no different in essence from those needed to kiss the barriers at Monaco in a Formula 1 car. The physical effort is, for sure, much greater in F1, the sheer physical effort needed to keep your head level under four G of acceleration, deceleration and cornering. Listen to DC himself. 'You're never fit enough in Formula 1. They are

Leading the pack. DC in the PSR Vauxhall Lotus, getting used to the opposition swarming all over his rear wing (The Scotsman).

extremely violent animals to drive. They accelerate violently, they brake violently, they corner at amazing speeds.' But the basic skills, the honing of the desire to win, the discovery of the knowledge how to, are fundamentally the same. Karting is where you begin to learn them.

For those who have never raced, a few laps in a kart in close company with others gives the fundamental flavour of motor racing. Tuck your wheels into a bunch of young guys going for it and you can taste and smell the brake linings, the burning Castrol R from the exhaust — even, on occasion, dust and grit from the track. Perhaps the most lasting impression, however, is of the speed at which everything happens.

For those who persevere, there is an almost magical barrier to go through into a different time zone. For the onlooker, everything happens at amazing speed. For the novice, hanging on grimly for dear life, things seem to happen even faster. But for the seasoned campaigner, the mental and physical processes speed up so much that

he has time and time to spare even when racing on the limit, his brain cramming maybe three minutes of thought into a one minute lap. He is thinking a corner — maybe even a lap — ahead, his body preparing to cope with situations not yet in sight. It is the first, and maybe the most important, step to becoming race fit. But karting is only one small step on the long road to being fit to race at the very top.

David had the best equipment
and help that money could buy

Coulthard's first kart race was on a track called Cults. This was much nearer to his home but, sadly, very short-lived. He remembers little about that first race 'except I definitely did not win.' But he did, far more importantly, survive it. For no matter how many laps you do in a kart, or a car, timing your performance against the cold reality told by the stopwatch, nothing, but nothing, prepares you for the wheel banging, occasionally bone breaking, dash into the first corner of the first race of your life. DC survived it, and came away hungry for more. Soon he began to pile up the wins, first in the heats and then in the finals at the end of the day when there is a trophy to take home and, if you are lucky, a note of your name in *Karting* magazine, the monthly bible of the sport.

When you are a junior karter in Scotland, or Brazil for that matter, the first title you have to win is your national championship. Not only does this normally win you the right to run a distinctive racing number — in the case of Scots, the distinctive letter S in place of a number — but it also gets you in the record book. Coulthard's first attempt at winning the Scottish Junior Championship took place in the autumn of 1982 at Rowrah, an English track so close to the border that it is regarded as more Scottish than English. When the Coulthard clan arrived there David already had a number of wins under his belt and, thanks to father Duncan, the best equipment and help that money could buy.

Given the aforementioned odds, what happened that weekend

Right *At the wheel of father Duncan's new Renault Williams — an exact replica of the truck used by the team to take the cars to races* (The Scotsman).

deserves a special place in the great book of motor racing history. For, lined up against DC was another teenager, Allan McNish, who would also make it into Formula 1 albeit, by the start of the 1995 season, only as a test driver. The year before Coulthard made his karting debut, McNish had swept the boards at virtually every meeting in the UK. Like Coulthard, and at an age when most children are still contemplating the change from three to two wheel pedal power, McNish had received a motorbike as a present from a father keen on motorsport. A typical cocky wee Scot, and a year older than the gangling, six foot tall Coulthard, McNish went on to dominate the UK for the next year. And as often as not, the results recorded 1 A. McNish, 2 D. Coulthard — then the rest. McNish remembers it well. 'Our fathers knew each other fairly well so we sort of hung around a lot. I remember David as being very fast, very smooth but, at that stage, not particularly aggressive.' (Later, after McNish had gone on to Formula Ford single seaters, and Coulthard ruled the karting roost, another driver destined for the top would play second fiddle to Coulthard's winning streak. Dario Franchitti, a works driver in the 1995 Mercedes German touring car team, would in turn take over the mantle from Coulthard.)

He believed if you were going to do something, you did it well

Tom McLaren, a former karting champion who now runs his own racing team as well as holding the karting concession at Knockhill circuit, was sponsor of the Scottish Championships at Golspie in 1985. 'I remember David as being technically very correct. He was fast and he was smooth. But it was McNish that showed the real flair. He had a style and a panache, while David always seemed to be chasing him. McNish was the driver that other drivers, those not racing in a particular event, would gather to watch at the first corner.' Coulthard's aggression, the real aggression that takes you through to the front of a Formula 1 pack, would come much later. But the boy was determined. And like his father he believed that if you were going to do something, you did it well. You never dropped below your own standards.

The following year, at Rowrah, Coulthard was hoping to consolidate his first round lead in the 1986 Superone series — then effectively karting's Formula 1. The rain was pouring down and the track was awash. The previous night had been wetter than anyone remembered. On race day, a Sunday, conditions were so bad that by the time the Superone final came round the light was fading. Coulthard, starting from pole, was overtaken on the first corner. He fought back, in awful conditions when all he could see was a wall of spray in front but, after trying too hard, lost it and spun the kart to a halt. The engine died because a class one racing kart has no clutch, simply a direct chain drive from a sprocket on the engine to another sprocket on the rear axle.

To start a stalled kart single-handed, you place one hand, usually the right, on the top of the steering wheel, lift the rear of the kart (the kart weighs around 150 lbs) with the left hand, then run for 10 yards or so while crouched over and carrying the rear. Finally, when you have picked up enough speed you drop the rear end of the kart and, in one fluid motion, jump into the driver's seat and operate the throttle hoping to start a high revving engine from impossibly low revs. For a fit adult, on an empty track on a dry day, restarting on your own is something to be specially proud of. Coulthard, a 15-year-old on a crowded track in the pouring rain, restarted his kart and set off to catch the pack, now half a lap ahead. *He won the race — on the last lap, within sight of the flag.*

Did Duncan, or more likely Joyce, teach him a lesson once? You never, ever give up.

Following his defeat at the hands of McNish in the 1982 Championships, David Coulthard was Scottish Junior Kart Champion in 1983 and 1984. In 1986 and 1987 he was Scottish Open Champion and British Superone Champion. In 1988 he was Scottish Open Champion for the third season in a row. But by the time the Scottish winter set in at the end of 1988, bigger things were beckoning.

The next step on the path towards Formula 1 was about to be taken.

CHAPTER FOUR

Cold as hell but fast as fury

KNOCKHILL RACE CIRCUIT in Fife is Scotland's only dedicated racing circuit. Set in the hills overlooking the world famous Forth bridges, the track is just over a mile long and, if it resembles any other track in the world, it is Brands Hatch. This is partly because it twists and curves over the natural contours of the land, partly because spectators can see most of the track from any one vantage point. Circuit owner Derek Butcher — a champion motorcycle racer turned successful single seater and now a saloon car racer — has built the circuit from a once-a-month operation into a thriving motorsport and corporate entertainment complex open for much of the year.

The only drawback to Knockhill, apart from its remoteness for most UK racing drivers, is that it can be one of the coldest, most miserable places in Scotland. There is no racing over the winter months, therefore. But corporate entertaining continues, with companies bringing their clients to try a variety of activities such as karting, buggy racing, or driving a rally car. All this takes place alongside a continuous programme of improvements and refurbishments to the track and facilities.

Right *Knockhill Race Circuit in Fife, where Coulthard first made the jump from karts to single-seater racing cars* (The Scotsman).

Main picture *Thruxton, March 1989. Used to winning in karts, Coulthard pulls on his fire resistant balaclava for the first time in a motor race and ponders the next stage in his career.*

Inset *David Leslie junior. He described his new protege David Coulthard as Good, a rare compliment (The Scotsman).*

Derek Butcher is a successful businessman. But he is also an enthusiast, and when occasionally he receives a call in the middle of winter asking if, perhaps, a new young driver can use the track to try out a car away from prying eyes, he can only give one answer. David Coulthard, after four years as a karting champion, arrived at Knockhill in November 1988 to drive a single seater racing car for the first time in his life. It was crucial to see whether he could make the jump from karts to racing cars. Not every successful karter can.

With him were two men called David Leslie. David Leslie senior is one of the gentlemen of motorsport who lavished upon his son David the same sort of attention Duncan Coulthard was lavishing on his own boy, but with a far smaller budget and a lot more technical expertise. The Leslie family had recently started their own racing team to run promising drivers in the junior formulae. Allan McNish was their first client, and he had swept the boards first in Formula Ford, then in Formula Vauxhall Lotus. Two years later, David Coulthard was their second client, his father reputedly having paid them a five-figure sum to fund the season.

But before that, a word about David Leslie junior who in 1995 is racing the works Honda Accord in the British Touring Car Championship. A former multiple kart champion, Leslie was born in Dumfries but lived most of his life in Carlisle which is just over the border from Scotland and, depending on which side won which particular battle over the past thousand years or so, spent much of its history as part of Scotland. Despite history and current geography, David Leslie considers himself a true Scot, wears the kilt with pride, and doesn't give a damn who wants to argue.

After a successful career in karting Leslie junior moved into single-seaters then, when he did not get the breaks into Formula 1, went sportscar racing with his national team, Ecurie Ecosse, and took them to victory in the 1986 World Championship for Class Two sportscars. And if anyone for one moment thinks that Leslie in particular, and sportscar drivers in general are not real racers, ponder this. In the 1983 British Formula 3 Championship which was won by Ayrton Senna from Martin Brundle after what was to go down in history as one of the classic seasons in that formula, David Leslie was the only other driver to take a pole position. He did this at Silverstone, then the fastest circuit in the world, and did it in a car that was desperately

'He's down to earth, straight-forward, honest and, well, just likeable.'

Coulthard leading the Formula Vauxhall Lotus race at Silverstone in 1990.

In 1991 he helped establish Paul Stewart Racing as a major force in Formula 3. DC had a reputation for fantastic starts from way down the grid.

When it mattered, such as in the 1991 Formula 3 Macau GP, he could turn in a front row qualifying position.

Making the most of this by leading from the lights to the chequered flag.

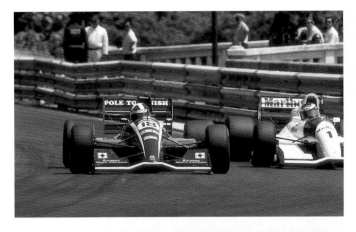

But victory on the streets of Pau eluded him the following year despite a spirited effort.

Silverstone 1994 seemed like the last chance saloon in an underfunded Vortex . . .

. . . but he finished second to Frank Lagorce (centre) after storming past Gil de Ferran on the grid.

*Barcelona, 1994. Making his Formula 1 debut
in a Williams Renault, Coulthard ran as high
as sixth before mechanical troubles disabled
the car.*

Main picture *Coulthard was given a second chance and a second F1 race, in Canada.*

Inset . . . *After cooking his tyres, he scored his first World Championship points by finishing fifth.*

Inset (left) *Coulthard's fifth race, in Hungary, promised much after he had set the lap record last time out at Hockenheim.*

Main picture *But after his only crash during a race he could only walk away.*

Right *Rubbing his hands after finding out he can compete with the very best.*

Below *'Nigel Mansell, in MY car, Frank? Och, come on . . !'*

In action at Estoril where he simply had to get a result.

Estoril, and the line-up went Hill, Coulthard, Hakkinen. Williams achieved its first one-two formation finish of the 1994 season, and Coulthard got the podium result he needed (ICN UK Bureau).

'I think I was capable of winning during the last three races.'

After his earn-ings jumped ten-fold when he signed full-time for Williams Renault for 1995, business manager Tim Wright became indispensible.

Unveiling the FW17 and its drivers.

Coulthard with his Canadian girlfriend Andrea Murray (ICN UK Bureau).

Inset *Brazil, 1995. Getting ready for his first timed session on a track he'd never seen, on a continent where he'd never been before, and him still recovering from tonsilitis.*

Main picture *Just two thousandths of a second separated him from his faster, more experienced team-mate.*

Coulthard eventually came second in Brazil, the only car to finish on the same lap as Schumacher. It was a victory that turned temporarily sour, however.

David and Damon. If Hill ever expected the young Scot to play the dutiful number two driver, he was in for a series of shocks.

Argentina. Coulthard led from pole at both the start and the restart . . .

*. . . and was
running away
with the race
until an elec-
tronic problem
put him out
after just 16
laps.*

*San Marino
Grand Prix.
One minute's
silence in
memory of
Ayrton Senna
(ICN UK
Bureau).*

*The fiercely
competitive
Williams
Renault team-
mates battle it
out (ICN UK
Bureau).*

Coulthard with his most loyal supporters, his parents Joyce and Duncan (Scottish Daily Record).

Many hands make light work (The Scotsman).

underfunded, woefully underdeveloped and, therefore, ostensibly uncompetitive.

Leslie junior was positive about David Coulthard's first attempt in a single-seater. 'We had ordered a new Van Diemen RF 89 but that was not to be ready until just before the start of the season so we borrowed an old Van Diemen and took David to Knockhill with that. The circuit had left the cones up from the racing driver's school and it was easy to show him the lines through the corners when I took him round the circuit in my road car. It was relatively simple, you simply kept aiming for the next cone.

'One thing struck me about David, he could learn new circuits very quickly indeed'

'We set the rev limiter at 5000 rpm, then lifted it by 500 rpm at a time as soon as his times had become consistent until, finally, by the end of the day we allowed him some fun by letting him use the full 7500 rpm and finding out what the car could really do. He was smooth, consistent and did not fall off. With McNish we had allowed him full revs from the start with the result that he fell off and ended up in the mud. Our mistake.

'Duncan made sure David did it right from the start. He got him into the car well before the season and we tested, tested, tested. Duncan had given us a respectable budget, nothing like what some of the teams were spending but what we considered we needed to win. We tested like mad throughout the winter on every circuit we could find. We used the old, borrowed car at first until the new one arrived, then, by the beginning of the 1989 season, we had tested at just about every circuit we would be racing at.

'One thing that struck me about David that winter, he was able to learn new circuits very quickly indeed. That ability stood out. We knew we were going to be quick when we arrived at the circuit for the first race of the season, but Kelvin Burt was there in the same class and he had been winning races the year before so he was definitely the man we had to beat. David beat him in the very first race. Suddenly everyone sat up and started to take notice.'

Coulthard made a deep and lasting personal impression on the

Coulthard takes the lead on the way to winning his first car race after passing Fennymore (30) and coolly outbraking Burt (95), the man he thought would be his biggest rival.

Leslies. 'He used to come down to the workshop in the evenings and at weekends and he'd take the car apart and clean it and polish it, and we would have to put it all back together again when he went home. This is in contrast to some other guys we have run who turn up every weekend and put their bum in the seat and that is all we would see of them. It didn't make David into a race mechanic or anything. But by the time he left us he knew what a spring looked like and what it was for, knew what a shock absorber was and how it worked.'

Neither David Leslie is known for suffering fools gladly, never mind prima donnas. Fortunately, they had no problem with the young Coulthard. 'David was extremely polite and pleasant. We have always had young racing drivers coming to stay with us all the time but David was the only one that ever stood up and volunteered to do the dishes. I mean, one guy turned up at the house and we brought him into the lounge and he picked up the remote control for the TV and started flicking through the channels. And we were all sitting watching the TV at the time.' Young David was also dedicated, missing out on the usual teenage pursuits to concentrate on racing.

Leslie junior knows how to race and, he has since proved, knows how to pick racing drivers. Not that he recognised Coulthard's potential immediately. 'I don't think David stood out as a great kart racer. He was driving a Zip in class one (non-gearbox) karts and Zip are best at making class four (gearbox) karts. I think the results that David had in his karting days were a reflection of his ability and owed nothing to the equipment.'

Coulthard was well prepared for the 1989 Formula Ford season. Before the first race — in March at Thruxton — David Leslie junior took the (for him) unprecedented step of writing to all the leading motorsport journalists telling them to watch out for the new Flying Scot whom Leslie described in typically understated terms, as 'Good'.

'How good?' we asked.

'GOOD,' said Leslie. From him this was thunder.

Coulthard, driving a bright red, Eternit-backed Van Diemen, won Thruxton in persistent drizzle. He got away third behind Graham Fennymore and Kelvin Burt. Fennymore, who had been on pole, was passed by both then, at the chicane on the first lap, Coulthard calmly outbraked Burt — and was never seen again. He won by 6.6 seconds.

Then he went on to win the next four races in a row — Brands

In a class of his own — the bright red Eternit-backed Van Diemen was a familiar sight at the head of any FF1600 race in 1989.

Hatch, Thruxton, Donington, and Silverstone — on his way to dominating both the Dunlop/*Autosport* Star of Tomorrow and the P&O Ferries 1989 Formula Ford 1600 Junior Championships. And the winning continued, in what was the most competitive junior formula on earth because, as everyone knew, this was the first big step on the motorsport ladder.

The climb towards Formula 1 is full of the improbable.

'Coulthard blitzed the junior FF1600 ranks — this one is going all the way'

The day before Coulthard's third Formula Ford race and third win, again at Thruxton, Nigel Mansell had scored one of the most improbable feats in the history of Formula 1. He won the Brazilian Grand Prix in a Ferrari that had hardly run more than a few laps reliably before the start of this first race of the 1989 season. Equally improbably, Coulthard was the man who would be chosen by the Williams Renault team to drive alongside Damon Hill in 1995 — in preference to Mansell, the 1992 F1 World Champion and 1993 Indycar Champion. But that was all still in the far, distant future.

Right now Coulthard was concentrating on climbing that motorsport ladder. At the third race, at Thruxton on Easter Monday, Coulthard, who had qualified on pole a full seven-tenths of a second ahead of his nearest challenger Kelvin Burt, went on to another win. *Motoring News* was already referring to him as 'the brilliant young Scotsman'. Then on to Brands Hatch where, although only second fastest in practice, he had become a teenage sensation in *Motoring News*. The paper described him as 'a star in the ascendant', enthusing that 'Coulthard blitzed the junior FF1600 ranks — this one is going all the way'. In the race he sliced past early leader Chris Goodwin on lap nine at Surtees, and that was it.

Occasionally, however, Coulthard could make an error such as at Cadwell Park on 3 September when, after taking pole from Kelvin

Right *1990. DC joins the Paul Stewart Racing team to compete in Formula Vauxhall Lotus. He is pictured with (from left) Gil de Ferran, Paul Stewart, Jackie Stewart and Derek Higgins* (The Scotsman).

Burt despite an electrical problem, Coulthard hesitated at the start, was overtaken on the line, then after seven laps of chase spun off into the catch fencing at the top of The Mountain. Cadwell Park? The Mountain? Once upon a time — a handful of years before, but half a lifetime to a teenager on a winning streak — another young charger who would make it into Formula 1 came to grief at the top of that very same Mountain. His name was Ayrton Senna.

Being named Young Driver of the Year came as a complete surprise

At the end of the 1989 season, with both Junior Championships firmly in the bag, the Leslies entered Coulthard in the Formula Ford Festival at Brands Hatch. Then the biggest international event of its kind, the Festival drew the cream of young motorsport hopefuls from all over the world. 'David finished third behind the works cars,' recalls Leslie junior. 'It was a very wet race and the works teams had adjustable shock absorbers fitted. We didn't. I know that if we had had the same equipment David would have done better, finished in the top two.' A note for the history books. In the 1985 Festival a certain Damon Hill finished third to a certain Johnny Herbert. Four years before that, a certain Ayrton Senna also won both Formula Ford titles, but missed the Festival when he decided to fly home to winter in his native Brazil.

A few days after the Festival Coulthard scored another win, only this time off the track. He was voted Young Driver of the Year by readers of the influential *Autosport* magazine in the first McLaren-*Autosport* joint awards ceremony. At the same event, McLaren boss Ron Dennis announced that Marlboro McLaren would back Allan McNish for the next three years. It was a gate on the road to Formula 1 for the first Scottish hope since Johnny Dumfries in 1986 and, before him, Jim Clark and Jackie Stewart.

The gate had also been opened for Coulthard. Part of his prize was a test drive in a West Surrey Racing Formula 3 car. But the best bit by as far as you can stretch your imagination when you are a young driver just barely onto the first rung of that awesome motorsport ladder, was the promise of a few laps in a McLaren Formula 1 car. He was to have very much closer dealings with McLaren at a later date, but that's another story.

To Coulthard, being named the first Young Driver of the Year under the new awards scheme came as a complete surprise. 'After I stood up I thought, "Did they really say my name?" As I walked to the stage they said that I was going to get an F3 test drive. I couldn't believe what they said. Then they said I get to drive a Formula 1 car.'

Afterwards, sitting with his family, Coulthard had a smile that was a mile wide. But it was not until later that the news really sank in. 'I went and asked Allan (McNish) what it's like, because he's tested one already. Now I can't wait!' But even in the elation of such a night, Coulthard retained his sense of proportion. 'I've got to keep my feet firmly on the ground. I'll just carry on with my racing and hope that I can follow in Allan's footsteps. He's got a fantastic chance there and I am sure he will make the most of it. As for me, well, I've got something to dream about now.'

Coulthard realised his dream in November 1990 when he became only the third person after Prost and Senna to drive the McLaren Honda. It was around about the time that young Michael Schumacher, who had just won the German Formula 3 Championship, took the apparently strange decision to move towards Formula 1 via the Mercedes world sportscar team. Coulthard too would dally with sportscars on the road to Formula 1, and would win his class in the 1993 Le Mans 24-Hour Race for Jaguar. But that was still in the future.

For 1990 Coulthard joined the Camel-sponsored Paul Stewart Racing team in Formula Vauxhall Lotus. The Milton Keynes team, which would go on to become one of the most successful in the world outside of Formula 1 and Indycar racing, was chaired by Jackie Stewart, three times World Champion. He believed in a very hands-on management style.

It was the first direct link between the Scottish Formula 1 glory days and the ambitious Young Pretender.

• CHAPTER FIVE •

Young Pretender
meets Old Master

FOR 1990, HIS second full season of motor racing, David Coulthard
had joined Paul Stewart Racing. PSR was set up in 1988 primarily to
look after the racing interests of Paul, elder son of John Young
Stewart, otherwise known as Jackie. But the team quickly attracted a
host of sponsors keen to be associated with, in the first instance, the
Jackie Stewart name. Right from the start one of Jackie's aims was to
use the team to set up what he called a staircase of talent to take
young drivers all the way from entry level formula such as Vauxhall
Lotus into, hopefully, Formula 1.

The team may have originally been regarded as something of a
joke by the cynics or, even worse, as a rich man's indulgence of his
son. But that would be forgetting what Jackie Stewart is all about
when it comes to motorsport — perfection.

Formula Vauxhall Lotus, known as Formula GM Lotus in Europe,
was a single-seater formula designed to take the place of Formula
Ford as the first rung on the motor racing ladder. In 1988, when it
was launched, the British series was won by Allan McNish, the Euro
series by Mika Hakkinen. After that beginning, there was never any

Right *Resplendent in PSR's distinctive yellow Camel livery, Coulthard has his
first taste of the big money backing needed to even approach getting into F1.*

question that it was the formula to tackle if you were an ambitious driver.

Coulthard joined the yellow-liveried PSR Formula Vauxhall Lotus team at the beginning of 1990 and, thanks to his multiple triumphs in Formula Ford the year before, started the season as a runaway favourite. But if DC expected another walkover he was in for a disappointment. This was delivered in the first race at Donington on 25 March when he was beaten by Vincenzo Sospiri — though he did finish well ahead of his team-mate Gil de Ferran who came ninth. It was not until Silverstone, fourth race of the season, that he was back at the top of the rostrum. Taking second place on the grid, he snatched the lead at the start after Shinji Nakano (Christal Racing), on pole position, was unsighted by the sun.

He was aware even then that a driver is only as good as his last result

---

Coulthard's Silverstone triumph was to be one of only two victories in the series that year. Even so he was just six points behind series leader Kurt Luby (K L Motorsport) when he went to Spa for a European series event — which was among the support races for the Belgian Grand Prix — to give him his first taste of racing abroad. With de Ferran concentrating on the European championship — he was lying a close second behind Draco Racing's Rubens Barrichello — Coulthard was happy with sixth place on the first lap when Swedish driver Kenny Brack tapped the back of the Scot's car and sent it into a spin. The rear of Coulthard's car just kissed the barrier but he came to rest on the grass, facing back up the track. Then, just as he selected first gear to move off again, Concept 3 driver Alain Plasch appeared over the hill, spotted Coulthard, and spun. The back end of Plasch's car hit the front of Coulthard's in a horrific looking crash but, fortunately, both drivers were quickly out of their cars.

'I spoke to Alain after the crash and he remembered nothing about it,' Coulthard said. He himself limped back to the pits with a very sore leg indeed. It was only much later, when he attended his own doctor at home, who sent him to the local casualty department in Dumfries, that Coulthard discovered he had a broken leg. Paul

Stewart remembers the Spa incident well. 'It was a really upsetting time for David and for his family. When they asked at first, the officials told them that he had been taken to hospital so they were naturally very worried as they thought it must be quite serious. Then they asked again and were told that he was back in the pits.'

With the next round at Donington just a few days away, and only three rounds of the championship still to go, Coulthard wanted desperately to race. 'If the decision was mine I would be back in the car at Donington,' he said a few days before the race. 'But I've got to see what the specialist says. I'm keeping my fingers crossed.'

He didn't race, and the 1990 championship was gone. Coulthard did however make the last race of the season, also at Donington, with no chance of the title but every hope of winning that race. He was aware even then that a driver is only as good as his last result. Coulthard made one of his fantastic starts from the second row and took the chequered flag at a gallop. Unfortunately, the marshals decreed that his start had been fantastic a fraction of a second too soon, so he was disqualified. By then, however, Coulthard was committed to a full 1991 season of Formula 3 with the same PSR team.

Coulthard's Formula Vauxhall Lotus debut in 1990 was disappointing, following his triumphs in FF1600 a year earlier, but he could usually beat his team-mate Gil de Ferran.

Recalling Coulthard's arrival at the team, Paul Stewart says, 'One thing I remember is that with David Leslie the year before he had been allowed to turn up at the workshops and handle the car. We didn't allow that and had to persuade him to leave the car alone and let the engineers and the mechanics work on with it.'

A word now, perhaps, about Paul Stewart.

Paul, a child of the original jet set, was brought up in Scotland and Switzerland, then educated in the United States. Like many sons of famous racing drivers of the sixties — Damon Hill, son of Graham; Geoffrey, Gary and David Brabham, sons of Sir Jack; Michael Andretti, son of Mario — Paul wanted to go motor racing, just like his dad. Unlike certain sons who were actively encouraged to take up the sport, however, Paul faced the wrath of his mother Helen if he even dared think about motor racing as a career. Equally formidable

Left *Coulthard's time at PSR introduced him to the professionalism expected by team Chairman Jackie Stewart throughout the higher ranks of the sport.*

Below *And he is off, through the first corner madness, already in the lead and going away.*

Two young Scotsmen on the make. Paul Stewart is contesting Formula 3000 but he expects David to bring the team the prestigeous British Formula 3 title.

was the wrath of father, Jackie, who may be referred to (but only behind his back, and only in Scotland, and only by those who know him) as Wee Jake, but is nevertheless one of the most formidable personalities you could hope to meet. Especially when there's money involved.

If Jackie Stewart is your father and decides that you will get a proper education and put such fripperies as motor racing behind you, then that is what you do. At least until you have finished the proscribed education. Paul was effectively barred from motor racing until he was 22 years old. In motor racing terms — the terms dictated by people like Senna and Prost and, well just about everyone else in Formula 1 — he was effectively an old man before he had even begun.

Aged 21 Allan McNish, then the great Scottish hope, was already testing Marlboro McLarens for Ayrton Senna and Alain Prost. Two years earlier he had become the youngest ever winner in Formula

3000 and on the way posted the fastest lap ever recorded in the formula. At 22 David Coulthard was a freelance Williams Renault test driver and poised to take his place in Formula 1. But Paul Stewart was undaunted. Faced with such competition from his home country — he was born and brought up in Scotland until Jackie discovered the tax advantages of living in Switzerland — never mind the competition from the rest of the UK, Europe and the world, Paul decided to go racing at the age of 22.

As if that was not enough of a handicap for a budding Formula 1 driver, consider this. At the time Paul decided to enter motor racing his father, three times World Champion, was still, in terms of Grand Prix wins, the most successful Formula 1 driver in history.

Ponder the 22-year-old son of this famous father going out, alone in the car, and mixing it with younger, leaner, hungrier drivers with 10 or more years experience behind them. These guys do not take

Coulthard waits for the start of his first F3 race in 1991. The TV camera mounted behind his head would record some of the most dramatic film ever taken in the formula as he powered his way into the lead, often from far back on the grid.

Inset *Team-mate Gil de Ferran had to become used to finishing second best, but the two remain firm friends.*

Main picture *Donington 1991 and after taking the lead on the first lap Coulthard realises he really can beat them all.*

Main picture *Coulthard rarely started on the front row of a Formula 3 grid but he often led into the first corner . . .*

Inset *. . . and when he did not, he then usually went around the outside at the next corner.*

Despite the astonishing first lap performances, he was always smooth, undramatic . . .

. . . except when enjoying his favourite drink.

prisoners. Paul Stewart went out there and battled with them in Formula Ford, Formula 3 and Formula 3000. And he sometimes won. Courage and determination were qualities he had in plenty. Also, like his father, he demonstrated a shrewd knowledge of what the market required off the track too.

PSR's aim was to create a rounded, all-in driver, a programme initiated by Jackie and nicknamed The Jackie Stewart Charm School. To this day Coulthard vehemently denies that his polished performances in front of sponsors and the media are a result of indoctrination. Paul explains the Charm School philosophy: 'The drivers go to learn how to speak in public and how, for instance, to talk to the radio in a different way to the way they talk to the TV. They really are different types of media and require to be handled differently if you are to do your best. We also tried to make sure our drivers knew how to present themselves. It is no accident that we have Boss (the designer clothing company) as one of our sponsors, because we believe you've got to get the whole package right. Just the smallest, unintentional detail wrong and it could mean that someone gets completely the wrong impression of you.'

In 1991 Coulthard came close to bringing PSR the F3 title it so coveted

In 1991 Coulthard would come tantalisingly close to bringing PSR the F3 championship the team so coveted, only to lose the title to Rubens Barrichello in the last race when the Scot had to retire after becoming involved in a shunt with Hideki Noda (Alan Docking Racing). But it was to prove a memorable year for the young Scot anyway. And one race in particular, the third round of the championship at Donington in April, was to play a crucial part in building his image. Not just what others thought of him, but how he actually perceived himself.

'David seemed to have this inability to put in a fast qualifying lap and often started from the third or fourth row of the grid,' Paul recalls. 'But then he'd make these fantastic starts and just drive past the people in front. Normally when someone starts from seventh or eighth in Formula 3 you think it will be a good day if they manage a

Left *Sometimes, when he knew it really mattered, he could pull out a first row qualifying position, and really make it count.*

podium finish. With David you knew he could probably win.'

At Donington Coulthard started from fourth and won the race on one glorious lap. It was one of the most memorable laps ever seen at the circuit — until, two years later, Ayrton Senna did almost exactly the same thing there in the F1 European Grand Prix.

Coulthard was fourth on the grid behind Rickard Rydell in the TOMs Toyota which had dominated the early part of the season, eventual title winner Rubens Barrichello, and Spanish Formula 1 hope Jordi Gene driving a West Surrey Racing Ralt-Mugen. At the lights he was off, fast as a thief and — going into Redgate for the first time, that long horseshoe shaped corner which can catch out so many drivers — Coulthard had already dismissed Barrichello and Gene, and was sitting on the gearbox of Rydell. Between the chicane and Melbourne hairpin he simply drove past Rydell and was never seen again.

'That Donington race was the one when I realized that I could beat them all,' he recalled. 'I went for it at the start and even before I had crossed the finishing line for the start of the second lap I was saying to myself that I really could beat them all and it was so easy.'

Coulthard won the next round at Brands Hatch. At Silverstone in June, he had another blinder, starting from seventh on the grid but up to second place by Copse on the first lap, then he took the lead going into Becketts and was never seen again. In the eighth round, also at Donington, he seemed ready to do it all again. He was into the lead by the first corner despite starting from the second row of the grid, but then his gearbox jammed and sidelined him for the rest of the race. He took his fourth win of the season at Snetterton then, just to reinforce his mastery, nipped over to Zandvoort to win the Marlboro Masters of Formula 3 race. It was the fifth time he had beaten Barrichello fair and square, to the one time the young Brazilian had beaten him.

Back at Silverstone again, Coulthard made his debut on the front row of a Formula 3 grid. After fourth place at Donington in April, when he was involved in a clash on the first lap, and a mechanical failure at Donington in September, he went into the championship

Left *Victory was Coulthard's in the Macau GP but for this shot he is behind team-mate Gil de Ferran for a change.*

decider at Thruxton needing a win to get the title — providing Barrichello finished fourth or worse. The Brazilian started from pole, Coulthard from seventh which for him was perfect . . . until he tried overtaking Noda for second place and had part of his rear wing knocked off for his trouble, costing him the race.

Apart from his fantastic starts, and his almost Senna-like ability to go flat out from the green light, Coulthard also displayed the first signs of a truly adult racer.

Anyone who hadn't taken him seriously before did so after this F3 season

---

Leading the non-championship event at Spa under great pressure from Jordi Gene, the Scot went into a sweeping left-hander going a little too fast. The car twitched under braking and started to run wide, opening up a gap through the inside for Gene who was sitting on his gearbox. Young drivers, especially ambitious young drivers in Formula 3, always go for the inside gap. But in the fraction of a second it took to realise he had left his braking too late Coulthard was busy working it out. 'I'd followed him (Gene) through there in practice and noted that he tended to take a wide line. When I made the mistake I realised it would feel really unnatural to him to go down the inside and I didn't try to defend the place, just concentrated on the exit line from the corner.'

'That whole season was a very important year for us,' Paul Stewart recalls. 'Up until then Dick (Bennetts, boss of West Surrey Racing) was the man to beat and we really wanted to beat him. We came so close. I think it was then that people started to talk about Paul Stewart Racing more seriously.'

Anyone who hadn't taken David Coulthard seriously before was certainly doing so after this Formula 3 season — especially his by now legendary starts. Especially when he won his very first 'Grand Prix'.

The Formula 3 Macau Grand Prix is not of course a Grand Prix in

'See how close I can get to the barriers at 140 mph.' The sort of picture mother Joyce probably preferred not to see.

the proper sense, any more than the Formula 3000 Pau Grand Prix earns a place on the calendar of the absolute top level of motorsport. But — fought out on the street circuit of one of the richest little pieces of real estate in the world — it was the perfect, high visibility race for the young up and coming driver on the make. Ayrton Senna won the race in 1983.

J.M. Barrie, Scottish born author of *Peter Pan*, is credited with the great line that 'there is no sight more impressive in the whole of the world than that of a Scotsman on the make.' Coulthard flew into Macau after the disappointment of losing the Formula 3 Championship and was very definitely on the make.

In the previous year's GP, the 37th, Michael Schumacher emerged victorious after an epic battle with Mika Hakkinen in a two-heat event which was as much a test of psychology as it was of speed. Perhaps realising the need to qualify well on a street circuit, Coulthard was second fastest behind Rickard Rydell. It took him one and a half laps to get past the Swede. Then he was gone, again. In the second heat, with nearly 10 seconds in hand, he was mature enough to give way to Jordi Gene who lunged past him on the outside at Statue Corner, knowing he could comfortably shadow him all the way to the line.

For any ambitious young racing driver the Macau Grand Prix is a gold star for the all-important c.v. For Coulthard, struggling to put together his Formula 3000 budget for the following season, it meant some money in the bank.

It was in this 1991 Formula 3 season that Paul Stewart believes Coulthard really found his aggression. Strangely, Allan McNish believes this did not really manifest itself until later, in Formula 3000. 'Put it this way,' said Paul, 'you do not win Formula 3 races from the fourth row of the grid unless you are really aggressive.'

• CHAPTER SIX •

Wheel to wheel with the boss

THE NEXT SEASON, 1992, David Coulthard joined Paul Stewart in Formula 3000 as his team-mate which, when you think about the importance drivers place on beating their team-mates, could have been a recipe for disaster. It is, after all, one thing beating your team-mate, quite another protocol beating a team-mate who is also your boss.

'We never really had any problems with it at all,' recalls Paul. 'I was very much the newcomer in motor racing, I was 22 years old when I had my first race, and I knew I had so much to learn from people like David and Gil (de Ferran) who had been racing since they were children.'

Paul's partnership with Coulthard in the PSR Formula 3000 effort was not, Paul now admits, all that successful as they had the right chassis but, until the F3000 Judd engine finally came good, the wrong engine. In such circumstances, when losing, or at least not winning, tempers can fray and occasionally snap. But the nearest these two came to a clash was at a pre-season test session at Jerez when Paul, on a slowing down lap, suddenly moved over at a place where, he now concedes, another driver might not expect him to. Coulthard, on a hot lap, nearly collected his team-mate and afterwards made his feelings perfectly clear.

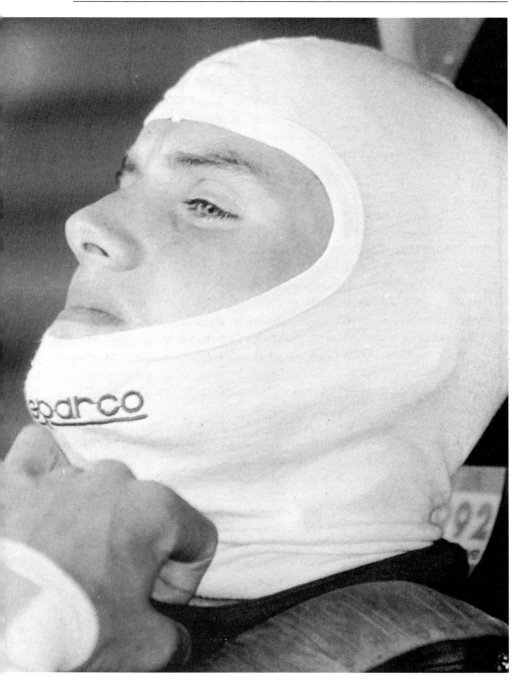

Left *1992. Getting ready for his first Formula 3000 race. Almost, but not quite, the big time.*

'It was quite heated at the time,' says Paul. 'But I explained what I had been trying to do and why I'd done it, and that was really that. Looking back on it now, it's almost quite funny.'

Stewart's easy acceptance of the possibility that his team-mate might beat him was perhaps understandable considering that, providing they did not take each other off, he was in a no-lose situation. If he beat Coulthard, so much to the good. But if Coulthard beat him it was the PSR team doing well. And while it is Paul's name above the door and he who has hands-on control of the day to day running of the team Jackie, as Chairman, remains the real power behind the Milton Keynes throne.

Someone, perhaps one of his sons, once encapsulated Jackie's approach to motor racing in a lovely piece of mimicry. It was delivered in a voice that was JYS to a tee. Arriving late at a circuit where his Formula 3000 drivers were taking part in untimed practice, Jackie dons the headset and microphone connecting him with the circulating cars just, as luck would have it, as one of the drivers comes on the radio seeking instructions.

'What will I do now?' the driver asks into the helmet-mounted microphone.

'Go faster, go faster,' commands 'JYS' abruptly, before demanding, after pausing a moment or two for thought, 'Who is this? Who is this?' It was not, for sure, David Coulthard.

Both Jackie and Paul make no secret about their desire to take their team into Formula 1 but they are reluctant to do so without winning the Formula 3000 Championship, the one title which has so far eluded them. For 1995, in what is some sort of irony, they have hired Allan McNish to spearhead their efforts in the formula. The third Scot to sit in a PSR F3000 car was hired, in Jackie's own words, 'because the bottom line is winning races.'

Jackie Stewart remarked, long after Coulthard had left PSR: 'David was probably the best prepared young driver ever to enter Formula 1.'

Following his karting and Formula Ford triumphs, and his fighting performances in Vauxhall Lotus and Formula 3, David Coulthard's

You don't want to get too far out of line with 450 bhp strapped on your back, but that doesn't mean to say you can't ride the kerbs.

Then again, sometimes it is best to stay off the kerbs, but only by a milli-metre or so.

Formula 3000 debut at Silverstone in May 1992 was a disaster. He was stuck on the back of the grid alongside Hideki Noda while his team-mate Paul Stewart, in exactly the same car, was starting in sixth place. Even Allan McNish, on a virtually non-existent budget as Noda's team-mate in Team 3001, was two rows in front. But he too had his troubles.

'What had happened was that a thunderstorm had struck just after the qualifying session. It was a farce,' recalls McNish. 'I had spun off at Brooklands and was just standing there watching the cars go by when DC spun to a halt in front of me. It was ridiculous, there we were, the two Scots in the first race of the season, standing in the mud watching everyone else and feeling sorry for ourselves.'

In the race Coulthard finished seventh, just one place out of the points and, ever important, one place ahead of his team-mate Stewart.

After Silverstone, Coulthard retired at Pau, finished eighth in Barcelona, retired again at Hockenheim. This was particularly galling as the big budget PSR team was being regularly outgunned by the third Scot in the series, Allan McNish, whose drive for Mike Earl in the 3001 team was one of the thinnest shoestring operations ever mounted in the formula. The smallest Scot finished fifth in Barcelona and an excellent third at Hockenheim in the GP support race, but he was doomed to run out of money and miss the final two events of the season. He still, however, managed to finish eleventh in the championship, two places behind Coulthard but, for him, a glorious two places ahead of Paul Stewart.

After finishing seventh at the Nurburgring Coulthard and the Judd engine started to come good. He picked up fourth place in Spain, another seventh in Albacete, then two podium places in the last two events — third places at Nogaro and Magny Cours. This was enough to secure him ninth place in the championship and a reputation as the man to watch in 1993 even though, for the first season in his career, he had failed to win a race.

Unable to continue with the costly PSR operation for 1993, David and Duncan Coulthard fished around for the best deal they could manage with a reduced budget. They eventually settled on Pacific Racing then, as now, a team famed for occasionally achieving big results on less than big money.

Mark Gallagher, Pacific public relations and marketing man, has glowing memories of the young Scot. 'What stood out about David immediately was the great rapport that he built up, not only with the members of the team but with the other driver with us that year, Michael Bartels. You get drivers who simply turn up and drive, and they can convince themselves that it is them (the team) and us, or him (the other driver) and us.

'Suddenly along comes David and he's down to earth, straightforward, honest and, well, just likeable.

'I think he had a great advantage too in having a man like Duncan behind him because his father made sure that his feet always stayed firmly on the ground. The two of them were some combination. They appreciated that they had a tight budget, but they had a game plan and knew what they were out to achieve. They also appreciated — and not everyone does — that things can and do go wrong and that at some races nothing goes right on the day.

'If David had a fault it was that his qualifying positions never seemed to reflect his ability in the car. In a race he's one of the very best in the world.'

The first round of the 1993 season at Donington in May seemed to offer little hope of a better season however when Coulthard qualified a lowly 14th on the grid in his new Pacific Reynard, no less than 10 places behind his former team-mate Paul Stewart who was now partnered by Gil de Ferran. Coulthard, naturally, made one of his storming starts and was running as high as fifth overall when, on the final laps of the two-part race, his engine expired after losing all its oil pressure. It had, it transpired, been blowing oil all afternoon.

Then came Silverstone and suddenly Coulthard in the Pacific looked to be in with a chance — though, after qualifying ninth, he clearly had his work cut out, even with his reputation for lightning starts. Mark Gallagher recalls the race vividly. 'At the start he just went through them as though they were not there, passing on the left, the right, sometimes right through the middle. It was as if he was walking on water. He just has to be the world's best overtaker.'

Half way round the first lap he was up to fifth place right on the gearbox of Olivier Panis and with third place Paul Stewart firmly in his sights. On lap 15 Coulthard took third place by squeezing between the battling Panis and Bartels. Now he was on the gearbox of Stewart and stayed there for 10 full laps until his former team-mate made a mistake at Becketts, lost momentum coming out of the corner and dropped two places to Coulthard and the still hard-charging Panis.

'I have never seen Paul drive so aggressively,' Coulthard said later. 'Though I have to say he was totally fair.'

With de Ferran a comfortable 22 seconds ahead of the pack and cruising home, Coulthard could only realistically hope for second. He took it on lap 31 after second place Michael Bartels got snarled up behind a back marker. *Motoring News* noted 'Fastest Lap BY MILES, David Coulthard'.

The street circuit of Pau is, the drivers reckon, the biggest lottery in Formula 3000. It is also an intensely satisfying circuit to get right. For a Scot, there is also the historic significance of the fact that in 1966 Jim Clark won here and so, too, did Jackie Stewart in a 1968 Formula 2 race, effectively the same Pau Grand Prix.

Coulthard finished second again, this time to Pedro Lamy, and this time with Paul Stewart right behind him. Yet he so nearly blew it. With four laps to go Coulthard realised he had no chance of catching Lamy and elected to drop the pace by a couple of seconds a lap to make sure he would finish. He was well aware of the possibility of losing concentration by driving at what to a racing driver is the equivalent of a quiet Sunday afternoon drive in the country.

The reduced size of the Eternit logo on his F3000 car compared with his FF1600 racer illustrates the way costs spiral as you move up the ladder.

Prominent among the Scottish backers (Crookes Healthcare, Eternit, Aggreko, Highland Spring) another man called Coulthard advertises his road haulage company.

After starting ninth at Silverstone in 1993 Coulthard stormed up to second place making this view of the PSR Reynard Judd a common sight.

Going into the hairpin he locked up and the car ploughed on towards the barrier. Even in the milli-seconds before the crash, Coulthard remembered advice from his race engineer. In such a situation, Coulthard had been warned, he should hit the tyre barrier as straight as possible. He did, the steering wheel released itself and that was that. Or could have been. He found to his surprise that the engine was still running. Coolly replacing his steering wheel, Coulthard backed out of the tyres and into the race. He continued, more carefully, until the end.

Finally, in the fourth round, fought in the heat and the dust of the Enna circuit in Sicily, Coulthard rediscovered the winning secret. But it came only after he had been barged out of the lead by Pedro Lamy who then, poetically, spun off 200 yards later before crashing out of the race on the last lap. Coulthard's Enna victory was to be the highlight of the 1993 season, however, as he retired at Hockenheim with a broken gearbox, and finished a lowly seventh at the Nurburgring.

Spa, the circuit where little more than a year later he would lead his first Grand Prix, brought his last podium result of the year when he finished in third place. But this, because he was forced to retire in the last two rounds at Magny Cours and Nogaro, was where he also finished in the championship. Olivier Panis, the champion, and runner-up Pedro Lamy were by then bound for Formula 1. Coulthard took some consolation from finishing just ahead of Gil de Ferran, but the future looked uncertain. He faced the winter of 1993/4 with no money and no prospect of a deal for the next season.

David Coulthard had some exotic memories however, particularly of his first ever race in the dark — in the 1993 Le Mans 24-Hour Race. At the invitation of fellow Scot Tom Walkinshaw, architect of the 1980s Jaguar triumphs at Le Mans, Coulthard teamed up with John Nielsen and David Brabham to drive one of Jaguar's newly launched XJ220 sportscars in the GT class. Two other XJ220s were entered, one of them driven by Coulthard's former mentor, David Leslie junior.

The Coulthard trio overcame a catalogue of troubles which started with a pre-race scrutineering row and included the car catching fire, and later falling on David Brabham's foot when the jack collapsed at

The message on the rear wing was not quite true. Not, at least, in F3000.

Main picture *Jackie Stewart pointed Coulthard on the road to F1. 'It is all out there, laddie, all you have to do is to grab.'*

Inset *'I know,' said Coulthard. 'And I'm grabbing as fast as I can.'*

Coulthard took part in the 1993 Le Mans 24-Hour Race, driving this Jaguar XJ220. He and his co-drivers John Nielsen and David Brabham won their class, despite a catalogue of troubles (The Scotsman).

a routine tyre stop, causing him to miss the start of the race and take only a limited part in the driving. In the race, the car also lost an hour in the pits because of a fuel leak.

With only nine hours to go and four laps to make up, Coulthard sounded desperately downhearted as the team attempted the seemingly impossible. But they made it. It took exactly two hours, with the Coulthard/Brabham/Nielsen entourage carving 12 seconds a lap from the leader, Porsche. They retook the lead with three hours to go, and finished two laps in front. Despite finishing 15th place overall, the trio won the class for the Coventry marque. It was the new Jaguar's first race. 'I didn't appreciate quite how possible it was to recoup lost ground in racing like this,' said Coulthard afterwards.

Later, there was a nicely tangible benefit for an almost penniless Scottish racing driver on the make. Ford, which owns Jaguar, and which had earlier loaned Coulthard a Ford Escort Cosworth in return for some public relations work, said that while he might be searching for a racing car next season, he need look no further for a high performance car to use on the road. That benefit was timely. At the end of the 1993 season Duncan Coulthard had an extremely difficult conversation with his younger son. He told him that the family could no longer afford to support his efforts in F3000: David would have to do so by himself.

The young Scot had not been idle however. He had by this time already negotiated a full-time testing contract with Williams Renault, following a season of testing for the team on a freelance basis. This would at least ensure that he could pay his way in the Milton Keynes house he shared with his girlfriend, Canadian model Andrea Murray, and his school friend David Cawthorne. But a testing contract — even with a top team — is a big gamble for an aspiring young driver.

It could lead to fame and fortune, as in the case of Damon Hill who filled the seat vacated when Nigel Mansell moved to Indycars at the end of 1992. Or, as Allan McNish found to his cost, it could turn out to be a blind alley. Three years testing and developing McLaren Hondas for Ayrton Senna and Alain Prost, followed by another season as a virtual full-time test driver for Benetton Ford and Michael Schumacher had left McNish at the start of 1995 with no real job prospects despite having clocked up an estimated 20,000 miles in the most competitive cars of their day.

During the winter of 1993/4 David Coulthard courted sponsors and talked to teams. He was competing with a score of other young hopefuls who, because they could not raise the £300,000 to £500,000 required for a full season with a top team such as PSR or DAMS, try to negotiate the best deal they can for the minimum budget. If you are good — as Coulthard knew he was, and as McNish knew he was in 1992 — you can sometimes persuade a team owner to take a risk.

By the start of April 1994 Coulthard, entirely under his own steam, had put together an estimated £150,000 budget. This was comprised of some sponsorship, some of his fairly modest earnings as a Williams test driver, many promises, but mainly debt.

Just two weeks before the first race of the 1994 Formula 3000 season at Silverstone, on 2 May, he had signed with Vortex to race their second Reynard Cosworth. There would be no time for testing, no time even for much more than a seat fitting before the first race. It was a desperate gamble. But Coulthard knew that to win anything, first you had to start.

• CHAPTER SEVEN •

The first day in May

SEVEN LAPS INTO the 1994 San Marino Grand Prix at Imola, in a weekend already blighted by the death of Simtek driver Roland Ratzenberger following a crash on the Saturday, Ayrton Senna had the most publicly recorded death in history after his car came off the track at Tamburello corner and hit a wall. An estimated 500 million people around the world witnessed the crash, which was many times more public than the assassination, three decades earlier, of US President John F. Kennedy. Thanks to modern communications the awful news was known to people thousands of miles away before it reached some spectators at the Imola circuit.

Those of us at Silverstone that weekend for the first round of the Formula 3000 Championship heard the whole appalling scene described by the BBC's legendary Grand Prix commentator, Murray Walker. Anyone with a grasp of motor racing could see the crash was serious. (In the aftermath of F3000 qualifying, I was sitting in our new motorhome, idly chopping vegetables for the family lunch, and watching F1 on a ludicrously small screen when I saw the unbelievable happen.)

David Coulthard was at Silverstone driving for Vortex. I had left him a few moments before in high spirits because he had managed to qualify a virtually untested car on almost no budget in second place.

For the young Scot — as the official test driver to the Williams Renault Formula 1 team — Senna's crash, and death later in hospital, had huge significance. The Brazilian, greatest driver of his generation, had been a colleague at Williams, and he had come to regard him also as a friend. Furthermore, as test driver, Coulthard was *de facto* reserve race driver. Though he did not know it at the time, (or if he guessed could never admit it publicly) the events at Imola were to thrust Coulthard onto the world stage and change his life for ever.

But for the moment, Coulthard remained focused on his present career. Just hours before Senna died Coulthard, up to his eyes in debt, had qualified a fraction of a second behind his old rival Jordi Gene and a fraction of a second ahead of his friend, but rival, Gil de Ferran. In his hands, as he watched the Senna tragedy unfold on television, was a fax from the Williams team wishing him luck in what might well be a make or break race. The fax was signed by Ayrton Senna.

In a plush motorhome just a few yards away from mine, Jackie Stewart was doing what he does best — or at least what he has done best since retiring in 1973 after winning his third World Championship. Stewart was charming guests, many of whom had backed the PSR team.

The Flying Scot and Frank Williams, the man who would give him the chance every aspiring F1 driver dreams of (ICN UK Bureau).

Inset *After the tragic death of Ayrton Senna, Coulthard joined Damon Hill as a race driver instead of being simply a test driver.*

Main picture *Part of the deal was that he should also drive a Renault powered road car in his spare time.*

Among the opposition that Coulthard would face in the next day's all-important race was Gil de Ferran in a Paul Stewart Racing car. Coulthard finished second, ahead of his old adversary. At the press conference after the race, still stunned by the news of Senna's death, he tried to dredge up some of his normal dry humour. 'I could do nothing about the guy in front but when I saw it was only Gil behind I was not too worried.' De Ferran, a Brazilian, was as devastated as Coulthard. But he too tried to find some humour. 'When I was lying third I said, ah, no problem, it is only David . . .'

As it turned out, this would be the last time the two great friends and rivals were to race against each other, for a while anyway. De Ferran, after losing the Formula 3000 Championship in the last round, went off to try his hand at Indycars. But before that, for young David Coulthard, motor racing's ultimate summons was about to fall on the doormat.

The Paddock Club, on the top floor of the main grandstand at the Circuit De Catelunya, near Barcelona, on the Thursday before the 1994 Spanish Grand Prix looked like something out of a guidebook extolling the glamour of Formula 1. It was here, among the carefully laid out tables, that Frank Williams announced what so many people had been suspecting for some time. David Coulthard was to be promoted to race driver. Coulthard — still gathering himself after a high speed crash a few days earlier at Jerez, shortly after Frank had arrived by private jet to oversee testing — may not have realised the full implications but it was a mighty gamble for the team owner.

Faced with finding a driver to replace Ayrton Senna, in a car identical to the one in which the Brazilian genius had died, Williams could have been forgiven for taking an easy way out and hiring a stop-gap driver such as the safe but capable Riccardo Patrese to steady the team until the end of the season. Or, backed by the team's share of the estimated £20 million insurance paid out on the death of Senna, he could have bought out the contract of a top driver and bribed him to join Williams.

Main picture *Girlfriend Andrea Murray lends moral support before his F1 debut at Barcelona (The Scotsman).*

Inset *Coulthard seemed the cool, calm professional as he took his place for the first time among the finest drivers in the world.*

If money had been a problem, which of course it wasn't, Frank Williams might instead have taken a flier on an unproven driver, cheap to hire. In the event he chose a middle course. Coulthard was offered drives on a race by race basis. And if Frank Williams was concerned about his decision he never let it show. 'I chose David,' he quipped to the assembled press, 'because he has an absolutely gorgeous girlfriend!' For the ambitious youngster — the first one to acknowledge the luck of being in the right place at the right time — this was the chance of a lifetime, albeit only possible because of a great driver's death. For the Williams team, Coulthard's optimism and blend of humility with confidence gave a ray of hope in a miserable season.

For Coulthard the warm-up boycott piled on the tension

Outwardly, Coulthard seemed the cool, calm professional as he prepared to take his place in qualifying among the finest drivers in the world. As if driving the great Ayrton Senna's number two car on his Formula 1 debut was not enough pressure for a 23-year-old, external events added their own weight.

There was open war between Bernie Ecclestone, head of the Formula 1 Constructors Association, and Max Mosley, President of the sport's governing body, the FIA. On the surface this revolved around safety improvements rushed in after Senna's death: Ecclestone, representing the team owners, demanded more time to implement the changes, Mosley refused. At a different level it was seen by many as a power struggle for control of Formula 1.

The struggle was carried out, as are all such disputes in Formula 1, in huddled corners in the motorhomes lining the paddock, where multi-millionaires meet and gossip like housewives hanging out the washing behind a miners' terrace. The team owners, testing Mosley's resolve, held a boycott of the Friday morning warm-up. Only a handful of cars from the smaller teams went out. Not enough, crucially, for the 16 guaranteed starters needed before a Grand Prix could be run.

For Coulthard, already nervous that he might not perform, the boycott piled on the tension because it denied him the vital minutes and laps in a real Formula 1 car on a track he desperately needed to learn.

Between the half-hearted warm-up and the first practice session, negotiations began again in the motorhomes and a decision was reached. What it was, however, no-one quite knew. One team principal, only willing to speak off the record, drew a finger across his throat and announced, 'Mosley is out'. Max Mosley, the dapper Englishman in blazer and flannels, didn't seem to think so. He appeared in the press room overhanging the pits to explain his version of events. The explanation was of no real consequence then to the young Scot, except in one respect. Qualifying *would* start on schedule, the race *would* go ahead.

Coulthard was one of the first in the pit lane queue held by the red lights until the track was opened and qualifying could begin. 'In a way I felt calm once I got in the car and everything else stopped. You're in the car and no-one talks to you. I was in my own little world that I have got used to over the last 10 years or so.' Different pressures of course but it is still the same environment. You are in control.

Coulthard went out in the first qualifying session of his Formula 1

Allan McNish, also official test driver for Ayrton Senna's Formula 1 car, would become one of the most experienced F1 test drivers in history (The Scotsman).

career and was 16th fastest due to a slipping clutch. Not perhaps remarkable in one of the two quickest cars at the circuit but, for a beginner, not bad. Crucially, he was in the race whatever happened now. Sixteenth fastest in the dry. Although the fastest times tend to be set in the final session on Saturday, the first session, especially if it is in the dry, is vitally important because the final qualifying might be wet.

'David did not get the chance to show what he can really do today'

The pressure was now off Coulthard. Or was it? In qualifying, Andrea Montermini, on a hot lap, and absolutely committed as he came onto the finishing straight, lost control of his Simtek in that fraction of a second before everything would have been all right. Even seasoned drivers watched aghast as, seemingly in slow motion, the Simtek — travelling at around 150 mph — ploughed through the gravel track, exploded against a wall and, shedding parts every which way, spun across the track to stop at the pit wall where team members and press were gathered to watch the session. In the long drawn out anguish between heartbeats they scanned the wreck for signs of life, hoping for the best, but each fearing the very worst. *Another race, another death?*

Damon Hill, under harrowing psychological pressure after losing his team-mate Ayrton Senna, looked stricken and, for a few moments, seemed to lose all self-control. The Italian driver was rushed to the Medical Centre and examined by the doctor in intimate detail. Afterwards he joked, 'the doctors examine my head, they say it is full of spaghetti.' I don't think anyone laughed.

In final qualifying Coulthard pushed just a little bit harder but never too hard, and qualified ninth. In a season dominated by Schumacher in a Benetton Ford, with Hill struggling to keep up, ninth was a good, solid achievement. You can win a race from ninth, but no-one does win their first race. In the history of Formula 1 only one rookie, Giancarlo Baghetti, ever has. He never won again.

Right *The eyes have it* (The Scotsman).

Race morning brought another dimension. In the warm-up Coulthard was fourth quickest. Suddenly, almost in unison, a lot of people asked the same question — *who is this guy?* Coulthard knew. 'I was not overawed in the least. It felt so good. When I sat there in the untimed warm-up and was fourth fastest and saw my name up there with all these other names I thought, *that's me, I'm there. I'm in Formula 1.* I felt very relaxed with it.'

On the starting grid he was still ninth. For those of us watching who had known Coulthard for so many years, ninth was great, no problem. 'He'll take at least four on the first corner,' we told our colleagues in the press box who wondered who this new guy was. 'He always does that.' He took three, thrusting his car into sixth place on the opening lap, then settling down in a comfortable sixth place to watch the jostling between Jean Alesi in the Ferrari, Mika Hakkinen in the McLaren, and JJ Lehto in the second Benetton.

'I backed off a little while and surveyed the situation,' he would explain later. You get three guys battling for one place and there is always trouble, Coulthard knew from a dozen years of racing. 'Besides, I had never raced that many laps before (65) and wanted to just sit there and see what would happen.'

What happened was a succession of faults, caused by a failure in the electronic software which gradually disabled the Williams car. First the power steering went, then the throttle began to play up. Finally the gearbox started to go as well. At his first stop Coulthard lost a whole lap as the car repeatedly failed to get away. Eventually he got the reluctant Williams out of the pit and back into the fray. For a while it looked as though he was still on for an, albeit distant, finish in the points. In the Williams pit, however, they were taking absolutely no chances. Not just two races after Senna's death. Not with a 23-year-old in his first F1 race. Not any time. They pulled him in.

But he had done enough for now — perhaps more than enough. For once Frank Williams, who had originally put Coulthard in the car for just one race, made up his mind about something immediately. 'David did not get a chance to show what he can really do today,' said the team owner after Damon Hill had given the team its first victory of the season. 'He will get that chance in Canada.'

• CHAPTER EIGHT •

Mansell returns,
but not quite yet

FRANK WILLIAMS GAVE Coulthard the chance in Canada, two weeks later, and the young Scot took it. He qualified fifth on the grid on a track he had never seen before, just one place behind his team-mate Damon Hill who, in turn, was behind the Ferraris of Gerhard Berger and Jean Alesi. Pole position went to Michael Schumacher, still on a roll that would effectively carry him to the 1994 World Championship at the very end of the season.

Montreal, one of the friendliest Formula 1 tracks in the world, is also, for the teams, one of the most cramped. The normally spacious paddock area is limited to a narrow strip of tarmac behind the pits and garages. There's room for a couple of caravans, a few tables to provide hospitality for the visitors and sustenance for the drivers — and that, apart from a single lane of tarmac, is that, before the paddock tumbles sharply into an artificial lake. Just how tight things are was demonstrated in 1994 by the sight of a courtesy van which plunged into the water just a few yards from the Williams enclosure after the driver made a mistake during a three-point turn.

Take the lack of space, add the near 100 degrees of heat, and Canada is a place where tempers can fray. Additional pressure was put on both the Williams drivers as the word was out that Nigel Mansell was coming back. Lured by the political skills of Bernie

Frank Williams gave Coulthard a second chance in Canada, where he showed his true competitive mettle.

By the first corner of only his second F1 race, Coulthard was past his team-mate Damon Hill and off hunting for the Ferraris.

It was a superb performance and one to encourage the Williams team, still stricken by the death of Ayrton Senna.

Ecclestone and funded by the effectively unlimited resources of Renault, the 1992 World Champion would reportedly return to the Williams team for four races which did not clash with his Indycar commitments. Though only *The Scotsman* ran the story on the Friday before the Canadian Grand Prix, the rumours were flying round the pits.

'To my mind I was not making it difficult for him to overtake'

For Coulthard, with just one race and no finish behind him, there was the very real fear of losing out not only to Mansell but, if Frank Williams wished, maybe even to a succession of guest drivers to fill the Williams seat at the events Mansell could not manage. For Hill — thrust into the number one slot in those desperate days after Senna's death, but still openly, sometimes very publicly, underrated by a lot of people who should have known better — the fear was almost as bad. What if Frank Williams, in a radical move to rebuild the team, should elect to invest in the comparative youth of Coulthard combined with the proven championship winning ability of Mansell? We will probably have to wait a long time to hear Damon Hill's real thoughts on those dark days with Williams during the middle of 1994, but some of the pressures put on him went far beyond anything to do with gamesmanship, never mind sportsmanship.

Shortly after the start at Montreal there is a real old fashioned chicane which the cars, slowing from around 150 mph, have to negotiate with a flick right, flick left before the long, hard accelerating run to the right again. The Ferraris, their qualifying times confirmed, were coming good at last. Schumacher, surely, would be overwhelmed by Berger and Alesi first time into the complex. Coulthard, we knew, was always going to take Hill at the start. Always.

Somehow they all got through, Schumacher disappearing off into the lead, the Ferrari drivers managing not to take each other off. Then Coulthard, then Hill. By the first corner of just his second F1 race Coulthard was past his team-mate, perhaps the most crucial benchmark for any racing driver, and free to go hunting first for the Ferraris, then perhaps, just maybe, for the German in the Benetton.

Hot stuff at the British Grand Prix. Coulthard is fastest in the pre-race warm-up.

During the first dozen or so laps of the Canadian Grand Prix Coulthard learned, or perhaps re-learned, one of the most important rules in racing. It is one thing to catch the car in front, quite another to get past it. Time after time he lined the Williams up for a run at Berger's Ferrari, but could not quite manage it. In his enthusiasm, perfectly understandable — what would you do if you were given the chance of a go at Gerhard Berger in only your second race? Damn right you would — he overheated his tyres and started to fall back, into the clutches of Hill. Hill, anxious to get past Coulthard and off in search of the Ferraris, was not amused as, time after time, his team-mate appeared to baulk him. Time after time Hill was on the radio to the pits, beseeching them to tell the Scot.

With the hindsight of a season Coulthard could have and should have waved his team-mate past as soon as it became obvious — and nothing is so obvious as a Williams Renault Formula 1 car right up your exhaust pipe — that Hill wanted, *needed*, to get through. Eventually, the team gave the order. Coulthard waved Hill through. 'Towards the end I was holding him (Hill) up,' admitted Coulthard. 'But to my mind I was not making it difficult for him to overtake. I was just leaving it to him to try and overtake. Of course, I am not one to move over for anyone until the team tells me.'

Eventually Hill got through and set off after the Ferraris. Afterwards there would be angry words, for now he had a race to run, a championship to chase. What Hill did not know, could not have known — and in the circumstances might not have been too worried about anyway — was that his young team-mate was in physical agony. His right leg had gone completely numb and, in places, he was having to push his right foot onto the pedals with his left. 'It was the most painful race of my life.' The problem — an old back injury causing cramp — would take him to Willi Dungl's famous Austrian physiotherapy clinic for a course of treatment.

Coulthard finished fifth in the Canadian Grand Prix scoring two vital World Championship points for the team in the Constructors' title. After the race Hill, still smarting, perhaps with cause, rounded on his young team-mate to journalists. Coulthard, equally angry, rounded on Hill for talking to journalists instead of tackling him direct.

'I'm a racer and I felt pretty good after that race.' Especially in front of a home crowd.

Main picture *After receiving the now famous 'Hakkinen chop' in Germany, he posted fastest lap.*

Inset *Hockenheim. DC greatly impressed the men at Pacific with his pre-race sociability.*

In a team still stricken with mourning, Coulthard represented youthful vigour, determination, and hope. Frank Williams rewarded the Scot with a small Saltire emblem painted on the Williams race number 2 behind Coulthard's head rest. 'I had asked Frank jokingly before Canada when I could get the flag painted on my car,' Coulthard admitted. 'He said he would consider it as soon as I scored some World Championship points.' When the Scot turned up for testing at Silverstone before the next race, in France, the Saltire was there.

Coulthard spent his days entertaining the sponsors — it was a PR triumph

---

Only Coulthard would not be racing in France. Mansell would.

Taking a leaf out of Hill's book from 18 months before when Hill, then a test driver, had hung around the Williams pit in Japan and Australia just to remind Frank that while Mansell was leaving he (Hill) was available to take the drive, Coulthard went to Magny Cours and, as test drivers do on such occasions, spent his days entertaining the sponsors, shaking hands and making friends. It was a PR triumph.

On the track Nigel Mansell faded away after the start, parked the Williams long before the end of the race (some suggest it was His Old Trouble, gearbox) and flew back home to the US. For him the race had been a disaster. Yet it had started so well, so full of promise. Mansell had dominated qualifying, throwing the Williams round the Magny Cours track to the delight of Renault, the French company supplying the Williams engines, here in the middle of France with all their important guests present. Damon Hill, perhaps sensing his career might be on the line, drew deep on who knows what final reserves of character — and beat Mansell for pole in the final minutes. He beat him by the merest fraction of a second, even on the scale Formula 1 cars are measured by, but he beat him, Nigel Mansell, his team-mate.

It was a glorious lap, fast and furious and, even from the fanatical Mansell fans, it drew a mighty cheer.

But at the start, the first time Williams had monopolised the front

Hungary. Coulthard had qualified third and looked set for a podium finish.

Then he put the car into a wall . . .

Before this he was really flying.

143

row for a full year, Michael Schumacher angled his Benetton Ford between the two in front and simply drove through the gap. Hill finished second, thus keeping his championship hopes alive. In the commentary box, sitting alongside Eurosport's John Watson, Coulthard could hardly believe his eyes when he saw Mansell park his car. 'Tut tut,' he told the listening millions, 'I'm afraid Nigel made a wee mistake.' Privately, his microphone switched off, he was punching the air. 'YESSS!'

Such was the apparent ease with which Schumacher had got the jump on the two Williams drivers that the Formula 1 rumour mill began to grind out reasons why this might be possible. One of the technologies banned before the start of the 1994 season had been electronic traction control which regulated the power from the engine to minimise wheelspin and maximise acceleration. Was it possible that not absolutely *all* the teams had observed this ban? Might it also be possible, the more technically-minded pondered further, for those redundant parts of a car's electronic brain which had been outlawed by the new regulations to be programmed to, just for instance, allow three fast starts with traction control — start-up, rolling lap, and controlled start — before automatically erasing that part of the programme to avoid it showing up in post race scrutineering? Might such a thing be possible?

At the British Grand Prix at Silverstone, Hill and Schumacher filled the front row of the grid. Coulthard, denied vital time in the car for nearly a month, was seventh fastest, and this on a track where in previous years, in less powerful cars, he had been regarded as a master. Though he would later moan at some length about how long he had been out of the car compared with Hill (drivers always, *always* want to beat their team-mate most of all, remember) Coulthard pulled out his own little surprise on the morning of race day. Even before the start.

He was fastest in the pre-race warm-up.

Between half an hour and 15 minutes before the race was due to start, each of the cars barked into life and set off round the circuit for the dummy grid. One minute before the official start they barked into

Right *The DC look as Coulthard models some of the Savane range produced by backers, Farrah* (The Scotsman).

144

life again and set off on another lap for the starting grid. Then, as the cars lined up ready for the start of the race and, remember, the third start of the day, Coulthard's hands came out of the car and waved furiously. The car had stalled; the engine had died.

The cars set off for another rolling lap ready for their fourth start of the session. Coulthard, having failed to move off in position but with his Williams now restarted, would begin his race from the back of the grid. At the start, Hill beat Schumacher into the first corner and won the race. At the back of the pack Coulthard was having a terrible race, but great fun. 'I spun on the first corner after passing a couple of people from the start, then set out to work my way through.'

From the back of the grid he came sixth, and felt pretty good

By the end of the first lap he was up to 22nd out of 24 drivers, by the end of the second he was 18th, then 16th by the end of the third, 14th by the end of the fourth and 12th after just five laps. Immediately before his second pit stop, quite late on in the race, the young Scot who had started from the back was challenging Jean Alesi in the Ferrari for fourth. In fact he finished sixth, coming from the back of the grid. 'I'm a racer and I felt pretty good after that race,' he said, as if it needed saying.

Coulthard still vigorously denies that the stalled car had anything to do with any strategy to make Schumacher go round again for a vital, fourth start. 'No, definitely not. I pulled down on the paddle (one of two with which the drivers change gear) and the car just stalled. There was a hydraulic failure.' Coulthard's version is given added weight by the fact that his car stuck in gear towards the end of the race costing him his first possible F1 podium finish.

Next stop Hockenheim, Germany. AFR in mechanic speak: 'Another F . . . g Race'. But not if you are a Scotsman. Out on the back of the circuit, little more than half a mile from the start, there's a little stone cross surrounded by carefully tended flowers. It marks the exact spot where, on 7 April 1968, Jim Clark died when his Lotus

Right *Sometimes all you can do is sit in the car and wait* (The Scotsman).

'You're in the car and no-one talks to you,' Coulthard would say later. In the meantime, as at the start of this race, you are never alone.

Main picture *An
eye to the main*

spun off the track and into a tree in an insignificant Formula 2 race run in the pouring rain. Because of that tragedy, as big in its day as the death of Ayrton Senna, Hockenheim is no ordinary circuit.

In 1994 Hockenheim was to bring horror but, fortunately, no fatality. Millions of people all round the world watching the German Grand Prix on television witnessed near tragedy unfold. The Benetton Ford of Jos Verstappen was engulfed in a fireball during a mid-race refuelling stop. Somehow, mercifully, the young Dutch driver survived virtually unhurt, as did the mechanics who were in attendance at the time. But it was a close run thing. That blaze will be the abiding image of the German GP.

'I was starting to understand the car and use my own settings'

In fact the whole race was dramatic. Hill received a pre-race death threat, Berger achieved an emotional victory in the Ferrari, and Schumacher didn't win the home race he so wanted above all others. Oh, and Coulthard set fastest lap.

'I had an indifferent time in qualifying but in the warm-up I got the car working really well. I was starting to understand the car and starting to use my own settings rather than Damon's and I got it going really well with the better fuel load on board.' (Technical note. Though drivers can and do share settings for the car governing suspension and aerodynamic preferences, the differences in their driving style mean that they have to develop their own optimum settings. The differences may be only marginal, but in the search for a mere thousandth of a second a lap, they can be crucial.)

Any hopes Coulthard might have had of a podium finish disappeared at the first corner where the young Finn first demonstrated the now famous 'Hakkinen chop'. 'Hakkinen bent my front wing in the shunt. I came in and had it fixed, then went out and set fastest lap by something like eight-tenths of a second or something. I was really flying.' Wasn't he just? He was not to finish, however. Gearbox again. But he did post fastest lap, covering the 4.2 mile circuit in one minute 46.211 seconds. This was a new record.

The young Scot was making a name for himself off the track too.

Mark Gallagher, Pacific Racing's marketing and PR man, recalls the interest raised by the one-time Pacific driver. 'At Hockenheim we were entertaining a senior director of a major international fragrance company, hoping to get backing. He told me that he did not know much about F1, but that he had heard of a great new Scottish driver, he couldn't remember David's name properly, and if he could only meet him he would really impress his friends.

'So I went along to the Williams motorhome and told David there was someone who would like to meet him. It was just before he was due to go out, and he was all suited up and carrying his helmet. But he came along to meet the man, and spent 15 minutes with him talking all about himself and about Formula 1. Three months later we had our new sponsor.

'How many drivers would do that just before they were due to go out — and for another team?'

In Hungary, again a new track for Coulthard, he qualified third behind Schumacher and Hill and, with 18 laps to go, looked comfortable for an easy, if distant third place. Then he put the car into the wall. Even as the car crashed, however, Coulthard was on the radio to the pits. 'I don't know what has happened,' he told his race engineer, every bit the cool-headed pro. 'I'm going to wait until the car stops moving and then I'll walk back to the pits and work out what happened.'

It was the third time he had crashed a Williams. The first time was at Jerez in front of Frank Williams on the day the team owner had jetted in to tell the young Scot he would be racing in Spain. The second time was later in testing at Paul Ricard, sometime home of the French Grand Prix.

Of course the wags, and there are no shortage of these in Formula 1, quickly christened him 'Clout-hard.'

• CHAPTER NINE •

The difference between winning and losing

THE DIFFERENCE BETWEEN winning and losing, as electronically measured in Grand Prix racing, currently stands at just 14 thousandths of a second as recorded after nearly two hours and 200 miles of racing, a record set when Ayrton Senna crossed the line ahead of Nigel Mansell in the 1986 Spanish Grand Prix.

But that is only a stopwatch, a piece of mechanical wizardry without the ability to think, or reason or make allowances for the multitude of factors which affect human performance. Ask a loser and he might well agree with the stopwatch, probably will. Ask a winner, however, and you will get a completely different answer. Winning is all about wanting to win, about wanting to win even more than the next guy, more than anyone else taking part. Winning is about confidence, about knowing that you *can* win and therefore will win.

David Coulthard had been used to winning from an age when most of us do not even realise the meaning of the word. Winning in Formula 1, the elite of the elite, is the ultimate competition. Could Coulthard win at the very highest level? Jackie Stewart has likened winning to finding a key: find the key, learn to use it and you can produce it as often as you want. David Coulthard rediscovered the key, or at least was able to pick it up, and get the feel of it for a time, in his sixth Grand Prix for the Williams team. The setting was Spa in

Belgium, the track on which his countrymen Jim Clark and, particularly, Jackie Stewart had proved utterly dominant.

Spa is a long twisting circuit which winds up and down and in and out of the Ardennes hills, a track where the weather can be completely different within a couple of miles, less than a minute's drive apart. It is what drivers call a drivers' circuit. In the wet it is a circuit for heroes. Coulthard reports: 'I went there feeling a bit down because I had not had the results that I had hoped for but I was very, very quick in the wet.'

In the wet qualifying Jean Alesi, brave as a lion, took his Ferrari out and went half a second faster than anyone else. Coulthard, sitting watching the times in the Williams, thought, 'no-one can possibly go quicker than that.' Then the young Scot went out and cut half a second from the Ferrari driver's time.

Fortune sometimes favours the brave or, on a drying track, the lucky. Rubens Barrichello in the Sasol Jordan gambled on slick tyres for the last few laps at the end of the session and scored the first pole position of his career — at 22 the youngest driver ever to take pole — as the cars of the front-running teams fell into disarray. Coulthard, frustratedly waiting for the Williams mechanics to change his grooved wet tyres for smooth slicks, lost valuable time, rushed into the pit lane, then stalled in his haste and did not make a dry lap.

He finished fifth in Belgium but things were about to take a dramatic turn.

Main picture *Damon Hill, sharing the back seat of this classic Caravelle before the Italian Grand Prix, answers the question, 'Who is that Williams driver sitting beside David Coulthard?'*

Inset *Italy. 'I was gaining in experience and confidence all the time.'*

He started the race from seventh place on the grid but was into third place by the end of lap 3, then running a comfortable second behind Michael Schumacher on lap 12 — ahead of team-mate Damon Hill. When Schumacher called into the pits for tyres and fuel Coulthard, before his own pit stop, briefly led a Grand Prix for the first time in his F1 career. Yet he had not the faintest idea of what it felt like. 'I later found out but did not know it at the time because no-one in the team had told me.'

Every racing driver knows what it means to push too hard

Whether he would have been allowed to win, supposing he had been able to overhaul and stay ahead of Schumacher after making his own stop, will never be known. On the run downhill past the pits to the legendary Eau Rouge, Patrick Head, Technical Director of Williams, noticed a definite wobble on the rear wing of Coulthard's car. Once again Coulthard was called into the pits on safety grounds. A long inspection revealed that the wing was indeed wobbly. But, after consultation, Head allowed the Scot back out. By then, of course, the leaders were long gone and he did well to finish in fifth place, equalling his best F1 result so far.

In the ragged, final few laps of a race which he had briefly led and from which he desperately wanted to salvage a podium finish, Coulthard pushed as hard as he could. At one point, when he went onto the brakes for the infamous Bus Stop chicane, he found a very long pedal indeed. Instead of slowing, the Williams rammed the rear of the Lotus driven by Mark Blundell. Blundell was approached by Coulthard in the pits immediately after the race. Coulthard apologised and explained what had happened. Blundell understood. Every racing driver knows what it means to push too hard, especially if the eyes of the world are upon you.

Events in Spa, however, were about to take a turn for the dramatic, a turn that would virtually guarantee Coulthard would not be allowed to win in his remaining races.

An FIA steward, examining the regulation wooden plank beneath Schumacher's car, ruled it illegal and the German was disqualified.

The plank, a large sheet of plywood, 10mm deep, fitted to destroy any aerodynamic benefits from the shaped underneath of the cars, was one of a number of changes instituted by the FIA after Senna's death in an effort to slow the cars and make racing safer. A 10 per cent allowance for wear was built into the rules but any other deviation was regarded as a breach of the rules and the offending team, and driver, would be excluded from the results.

It seemed that Schumacher had lost Spa therefore. Coulthard moved up to fourth place overall but, far more significant, Damon Hill — 13.662 seconds behind Schumacher at the finish line — was now race winner. The 1994 World Championship, so long seemingly a one-horse race, was suddenly back on.

A few days later the World Motor Sport Council in Paris confirmed Schumacher's two race ban for ignoring the black flag during the British Grand Prix at Silverstone. The black flag had been unfurled to call the German into the pits for a 10 second stop/go penalty imposed because he had overtaken pole position Hill and not kept to grid order on the warm-up lap before the race.

Schumacher, of all people, should have known that rule for it is instilled in drivers from their very first race. On the rolling warm-up lap, the pole position man controls the pace of the cars behind, and there can be no question at all about it. In karting, as in Formula 1, the pole position man may choose to get to his position on the front of the grid as fast as he possibly can. Or, if he has a mind to and he thinks it might work, he can wander round at a snail's pace hoping that his rivals behind may overheat their engine, overcool their tyres, or perhaps simply foul a plug.

It is, unofficially of course, just another good reason to try to start from pole. Screwing up this most basic rule cost Schumacher potential wins at the next two races — Italy, then Portugal. If, in his absence, Hill could win these races, they would not renew the battle until the penultimate race in Japan, and then only one point apart. Coulthard's role from now on would be a bit part. His job was to score points for Williams in the Constructors' Championship and, above all else, to help Hill win the world title.

Monza is a track which stirs the very soul of racing drivers. If any Grand Prix circuit can claim to be the home of motor racing it is Monza, one of the fastest tracks in the world where, in 1971, Peter

Left *Coulthard, foreground, spins during the first corner mayhem. Later he ran out of fuel, but he still considered this his best race so far* (The Scotsman).

Gethin won what is still the fastest Grand Prix in history at an *average* speed of 150.755 mph. That was in the days before safety chicanes killed such huge speeds. Gethin won from three others all nose to tail after nearly 200 miles of racing.

For a Scottish driver, however, it possibly means even more. It was at Monza in 1965 that Jackie Stewart scored his first Grand Prix victory. The runner-up? An English driver called Graham Hill. It was at Monza that Jim Clark — even though he eventually lost — produced what is still, more than a quarter of a century later, regarded as his greatest race, one of the milestone races in the history of the sport. Clark had lost his lead with a puncture and fell a full lap behind the leaders during his slow speed trip to the pits and while the tyre was changed. He then came back, caught the leaders, unlapped himself, caught them again and retook the lead — only to run out of fuel within sight of the flag.

David Coulthard could not escape the sense of history that permeated the Monza track when he arrived there in September 1994 for only the seventh race of his F1 career. It was a race that just *had* to be packed with drama. He did not disappoint, for it proved to be the second of three consecutive events where he could have won, after surviving the first corner pile-up which forced the restart.

At Monza, Coulthard had what he considered his real breakthrough race because, finally, he went into the lead and, for the first time, knew it. 'I was looking very strong in qualifying because I was gaining in experience and confidence all the time. I was quicker than Damon in the first qualifying, then the engine blew up in the second session on my first flying lap so I ended up fifth on the grid.'

The record books — pole position, fastest lap, winner — tell some of the story of Formula 1, but they cannot hope to tell it all. Something akin to sibling rivalry comes into it too. Allan McNish sums it up beautifully. 'No matter what else is going on, your teammate is the only one with exactly the same equipment as you, and to a driver that is all that matters, measuring yourself against someone in identical equipment and winning.'

Coulthard was faster than Damon in the first practice. In his mind,

If Michael Schumacher can ride a bike, then I can ride one better — especially if there is a Scottish flag to back me up.

Even when things went wrong, he could manage a smile and a wave.

that was all that counted. He had *won*. 'In the race, my best race, I felt very strong, very comfortable, and I felt that I could have gone quicker than Damon. I led the race for a few laps, then they asked me to let Damon past.' If Damon was going to pass him, the Scot reasoned, then he could at least make it look interesting for the spectators. The team had other ideas. 'I knew that I would respond ultimately to whatever orders the team gave me and I was thinking about letting him past when he caught up. I could not have waited 35 seconds or something. I could not have made myself look foolish.'

But the team came on and said, 'let Damon past.'

'I said, no, he can pass when he is closer.

'They came back on the radio and said, let him past.

'I replied, not close enough, I'll let him by when he is closer.

'They came back on and said, look, MOVE OVER.

'So I moved over.

'But it was nice. I had had so many bad races with the car stuck in gear and times when I expected something to happen.'

Something did happen. The almost unbelieveable in a team like Williams happened. But he was not unhappy. 'That was my best race of the year. I was in control and well within myself. I thoroughly believed I could win that race.'

The unbelievable — 'I ran out of fuel.'

Watched by thousands at the track and millions on television, Coulthard unbuckled himself, climbed out of the car, then ran back to the pits. Might he, we wondered, be rushing back to discuss the finer details of weights and measures with the Williams fuel man? No, said Coulthard. 'I ran back to the pits because I saw the mood of the crowd, knew that Ferrari had not won and wanted to get the hell out of there before they invaded the track.'

Though Coulthard considered Monza his best race of the 1994 season so far and was happy to leave it at that, World Championship considerations of course meant that Coulthard had to let Damon Hill past. But something had changed, perhaps for ever, inside Coulthard's brain. Something not unrelated to confidence.

'You could argue that Damon was only racing against the third placed man in the race because he knew that I would have to let him past. So I am not foolish enough to think that he could not have gone quicker. *But I could have gone quicker too.*'

• CHAPTER TEN •

Sometimes coming second can be enough

COULTHARD ARRIVED AT the Estoril circuit near Lisbon knowing that he had to secure a podium finish in his last race of 1994 for Williams. The young Scot desperately wanted a result to help ensure that, when it came to choosing new drivers for 1995, the team managers would have him top of their shopping lists.

With Schumacher sitting out the second race ban and the self-evident fact that Damon Hill would have to be allowed to win the Portuguese Grand Prix to keep the championship alive, Coulthard knew that second place was all he could hope for. He knew what he had to do. Or did he? With Mansell scheduled to take his seat and no concrete word from Frank Williams for next season, might he simply just go for the win and to hell with it? Risk all on the big play?

In the Friday practice Hill almost made the decision for him when he wrecked his car during the second qualifying session after a spectacular roll — locking wheels with the spinning Eddie Irvine's Jordan Hart — trying to beat Berger's provisional pole position time. Hill, visibly shaken by the first occasion he had ever been upside down in a car, was, thankfully, unhurt.

Coulthard took provisional third place on the grid three-tenths of a second behind his team-mate and under a second behind Berger. The Friday line-up survived for the start of Sunday's race. Would

Coulthard, we wondered, emerge first or second from the first corner and, if he emerged first, then what? At the start the Scot surged past Hill and nearly took Berger before settling down to watch on Berger's tail. While Hill relaxed and worked out the tactics of the race, Coulthard started to push the Ferrari driver. 'Gerhard was pushing it hard at the start. I watched his driving start to get ragged as his tyres went off. Then I started to think about pushing him into a mistake.'

In his eighth race, the 23-year-old Scot was thinking of manoeuvring race leader Gerhard Berger — one of the fastest and most experienced drivers on the track, in a Ferrari — into a mistake. On the eighth lap the Ferrari's transmission packed up and Berger parked his stricken car neatly at the side of the circuit. Coulthard was suddenly leading and with a clear track ahead of him. It was an experience to savour.

'I was pulling away and leading a Grand Prix and that felt fantastic. I was leading, I was genuinely leading and the car was performing and I was doing the job. I was pushing, but I did not feel able to push with the same disregard as you do, say, in Formula 3000. In F3000 you pay your money and you do your job. In Formula 1 it is a fine balance

It was not until Estoril, in his eighth F1 race, that he would score his first podium finish, following team-mate Damon Hill across the line to second place.

Main picture *Perhaps a slight touch of nerves as he prepares to be announced as Frank Williams's choice for 1995 instead of Nigel Mansell.*

Inset *After the announcement, Coulthard faced more cameras than he had ever seen in his life before.*

between showing how quick you are and getting the job done to win the points.'

On lap 11, pulling away from Hill who was now a distant second, he set fastest lap. On lap 12 he beat his own time with what was to remain fastest lap of the race. By the first pit stop he was six seconds clear of Hill and, though he lost a second in the pit stop, was still well clear when they had both rejoined the race.

Coulthard's lead was to last until the 28th lap when, under orders to let Hill through, Coulthard moved over in traffic. He then dutifully followed his leader to the chequered flag lapping everyone up to fifth place, and helping to give the Williams team its first one/two formation finish of the season.

'No matter what the formula, when you want to win you want to win'

After the traditional champagne spraying on the podium where the Scot said he was happier for the mechanics than he was for himself, he was able to voice his thoughts on his F1 career so far. 'I've never raced with Schumacher (racing means wheel to wheel combat rather than simply taking part in the same event) though it would have been extremely difficult to beat him because he is so confident. I think I was capable of winning during the last three races. You've got to prove to yourself first that you can win. At this level a lot of Schumacher's time comes from his confidence.'

The podium smile belied his feelings. 'I was not as happy as maybe my face showed. I was happier for my mechanics than I was for myself because I wanted to be in that number one spot. It just made me realise at that moment that it does not matter what formula you are racing in. When you want to win, you want to win.'

No matter how hard you want to win however, first you need to take part — and in Formula 1 you need a competitive car which, most years, means a Williams, a Ferrari, a McLaren or, latterly, a Benetton. As he left the Estoril circuit for the half hour drive to

Right *With the Williams drive in the bag, DC can afford to smile at the opening of the Autosport International exhibition in January 1995* (The Scotsman).

Lisbon airport after the greatest success of his career, Coulthard had none of those. He had nothing, in fact, except his original testing contract with Frank Williams who had let it be known that the document included an option on the Scot for 1995.

Worse, far worse, Nigel Mansell was about to take over *his* car for the last three races of the season which, because the battle for the title between Hill and Schumacher was boiling nicely to a climax, would attract even more media publicity. It didn't help to know that for this service Mansell was reportedly receiving around £1 million *per race*, whereas Coulthard was still on a relatively modest test driver's pay plus about £5,000 a race.

Mansell, aged 41, was an old, old man in a sport which favours the faster reactions of younger men, but he was one of the greats of the Senna/Prost era. He had won the Formula 1 and Indycar titles in successive seasons and, even his greatest detractors had to admit, he was one of the great all-time chargers. Not to say crowd-pullers. Nigel Mansell, in the car, was Hollywood's version of how a real racing driver should be. Smoking tyres, locked brakes, wild slides, and corny as they come. Oh, and those mad, breathtaking charges through from the back of the grid, often to win. Renault, having won a world title with Mansell before, accepting he was a known quantity and wanting maximum media coverage, wanted Mansell.

State-owned, but soon to be privatised, Renault needed more than a knowing wink from the French finance ministry to survive. It needed image, sales and profits. Perhaps, since the retirement of Prost and the death of Senna, Mansell was the only big name star. So much the better, thought Renault.

To Bernie Ecclestone, who charges each circuit a hefty fee to stage a Grand Prix, a fee based on attendance as much as any other earning power, Mansell is simply money in the bank. An astonishing 50,000 more spectators turned up to see Mansell winning the British Grand Prix in 1992 than paid to see Hill win the same event two years later. At up to £300 a head for the full, three-day event, this adds up to a tidy £15 million extra income — from just one event.

Coulthard elected to attend all the remaining races in the 1994 season. With someone as temperamental and, we must assume, as nervous as Mansell during his much hyped comeback, the presence of his younger rival in the pits, the paddock, the motorhome, might just rattle him enough. Coulthard duly turned up in the pits for the European Grand Prix in Jerez, where Mansell, we understand, was not in the least amused. The Young Pretender also maintained the pressure in both Japan and Australia.

But even before the start of the European race, things were to change dramatically and, as always in Formula 1, at great speed. Responding to one of three messages left on his telephone answering machine from top teams within a matter of hours of each other, Coulthard had dinner at Jerez with McLaren boss Ron Dennis. After seeking the advice of his management company, IMG, Coulthard signed a contract of intent with McLaren which, we had just learned, were to have Mercedes power, and money, for 1995.

The move either forced Williams's hand or freed DC to join McLaren

Quite what the wily Dennis was up to is not yet officially recorded. Dennis is hardly the most forthcoming team owner. But the most popular theory was that he used the situation to test the strength of current contracts in Formula 1. Aside from a 'little' money in legal fees (a year or more's wages to most of us but simply loose change in Formula 1 terms) Dennis might or might not get Coulthard (whose dream car for the road, incidentally, is a Mercedes 500SL which naturally Mercedes-Benz would be only too happy to supply). But he would certainly get the measure of the strength of contracts. As a fringe benefit, of course, Dennis would also wind up his old rival Frank Williams. Rather nicely in fact.

And if Williams won, and McLaren lost the services of Coulthard on this occasion, well Dennis had probably caused the wages of the young Scot to be upped by a considerable amount and, well, there's always another time and surely Coulthard would remember to whom he owed a favour. Coulthard too could only win by this manoeuvre. The move either forced Frank Williams into coming up with a full season's racing alongside Hill, who had already re-signed for 1995, or it freed him to join McLaren which, in a new season, with a new engine formula and all new design, might well turn out to be a winner again.

Young Coulthard knows his own worth, and is undoubtedly canny in business. Throughout his racing career he has also been widely liked for being courteous, straightforward, and approachable. His regard for the people who backed his career, particularly in the early stages, is almost legendary. He inspires unflagging loyalty from those who become involved with him, as witnessed by the number of names — Crookes Healthcare, Eternit, and Highland Spring to name but three — who have stuck with him. This anecdote gives an idea why.

On the eve of the storm over his contractual wrangle between Williams and McLaren, DC spent an evening at an indoor kart racing centre on the outskirts of Glasgow with Farrah Trousers and their guests — sales people from Ralph Slater Ltd, the company which, according to the Guinness Book of Records, boasts the biggest menswear department in the world. While DC, resplendent in his Williams racing suit and famous Saltire helmet, took part in a seemingly endless series of kart races, between times chatting with sales staff, Managing Director Eric Thornton talked about what his sponsorship of Coulthard meant for him and his company. 'It was a straightforward business decision for us. It is not as if I or any of the directors are motor racing mad. But we believe that the range of trousers we produce for young people should be promoted by rising stars in sport, and David was one of the names we picked.' The sponsorship, reputedly around £50,000 a year, is a worthwhile investment, he feels: after every event like this, sales soar.

'When we first agreed the deal it was at the start of the 1994 season when he was driving in F3000. He was to model our trousers for some fashion shots, and turn up for a certain number of days during the year to events like this. Obviously now he has made it into F1 we could never even dream of affording the same sort of deal, but not only has he met all his commitments to us in full but you just need to ask him to do something and if it is humanly possible he does it. And he does it wholeheartedly. Turns up on time, meets people, is himself, and stays on for as long as people want him to.'

Shortly after this event Coulthard returned to Knockhill, the

Right *Strapped firmly into the seat of his own F1 car at last, Coulthard looks forward to his first full season of Grand Prix racing* (ICN UK Bureau).

circuit where he had first driven a racing car just six years before, to meet with the Scottish press who had backed him from those early days. It was only 48 hours after news broke of the contractual battle, and the first time we had been able to talk to him. This was the biggest media gathering for a motorsport personality since the days of Jackie Stewart.

Reflecting on the fact that it was barely six months since he had been just another struggling F3000 driver with big hopes but virtually no budget, Coulthard was in typically forthright mood.

'Have you,' I asked, 'signed any sort of contract with McLaren?'

He was silent for the best part of half a minute. 'Jim, you are the first person I have admitted it to. Yes. But you all know me. You know I would not do anything dishonest. You know I would not have signed something unless I was sure I was legally entitled to do so.' He then explained with great conviction, how he would be doing a full season of F1 in 1995 with a top team, whichever one it was.

He moved to Monaco, where the real big shots live

One thing about DC: ask him a straight question and you get a straight answer. The first time I met him was when he arrived in my office at *The Scotsman* early in 1989, shortly after David Leslie junior had tipped off the UK press about the potential of his new driver. Carrying the slim black attache case with the postage stamp size Saltire sticker which still accompanies him to this day, Coulthard sat down across the desk and explained that he was a racing driver and that he was going all the way. There was no rash talk of 'I'm the best' or 'I'm going into Formula 1' or the then current boast 'I'm going to be the next Jackie Stewart'. This was just a very confident, obviously determined 17-year-old boy sitting telling someone twice his age that he was going all the way. How right he was.

But back now to late 1994 and the contractual dispute. This would not be settled until after the season ended, and there were still three races to go. There was still the Nigel Mansell problem — and nobody underestimates Nigel Mansell in a race car, ever. Least of all Coulthard: If Nigel comes back and doesn't do very much then I'm in with a good chance. *But if he is blindingly quick . . .* The young Scot did not need to speculate.

Mansell spun off in Jerez. He got bogged down behind Alesi in Suzuka, though he did show some of his old fire in the dreadful conditions. Then he went on to confront his own personal bogey, the street circuit of Adelaide. There, eight years earlier, the near certainty of his first World Championship became a 200 mph battle for life as his rear tyre exploded at the fastest part of the track. The result of the 1994 title fight ended just a whit less dramatically. Schumacher crashed into Hill, the only driver who could take the championship from him. Mansell, who had started from pole, but fallen nearly a minute behind, won the race.

Frank Williams is notoriously slow at making decisions. Here he was faced with a thorny dilemma. It was a choice between the man who had won more races for him than any other driver, or a 23-year-old newcomer who had not even raced for a full season. Williams might have gone either way: the Old Lionheart or the Young Pretender. It was as finely balanced as that. But there was that challenge from Ron Dennis and, perhaps more important, dissent within his own team. The message loud and clear on the jungle drums which

The new kid on the block looked set to be fast.

reverberated through the team was *we do not want Nigel back*. Frank Williams gave his answer when he hired one of the UK's most accomplished — and expensive — advocates to argue, and easily win, his case in front of the FIA Contracts Recognition Board in Geneva.

The official announcement, originally scheduled for 1 January 1995, was delayed for a day to take into account the Scottish New Year. Nobody celebrates New Year like the Scots and, for one young Scot in particular, there really was something to celebrate. Coulthard, like thousands of other revellers, gathered outside the Tron Church in Edinburgh. It is, perhaps, one of the greatest street parties in Europe, one where the Scots really let their hair down and, some of them at least, get gloriously, uproariously drunk.

For Coulthard, 1995 already promised much. As a start, his basic income, he knew by now, was to increase ten-fold from around £50,000 a year to £500,000. On the strength of this he would move from his relatively humble house in Chiswick in central London, recently bought on the proceeds of his eight races with Williams, to a luxury flat overlooking the harbour in tax exile Monaco. It was the next logical step for the youngster who prided himself on having an organised life. Not that he was getting big-headed, or forgetting the recent cash flow struggles — but Monaco was where the big shots went.

Two days into 1995 Coulthard attended the hurriedly called press conference at Williams's Oxfordshire HQ. He was announced as the 'other' driver — the team stressed this, rather than calling him the number two driver — to partner Damon Hill.

Afterwards, following all the interviews, Coulthard toured the works and tried to talk to everyone in the place. It was the sort of gesture that some drivers might never have even thought of. For the Young Pretender, preparing to assume his countrymen's mantle, perhaps it was more than a New Year gesture, more a statement of faith.

You look after me guys, and I will look after you.